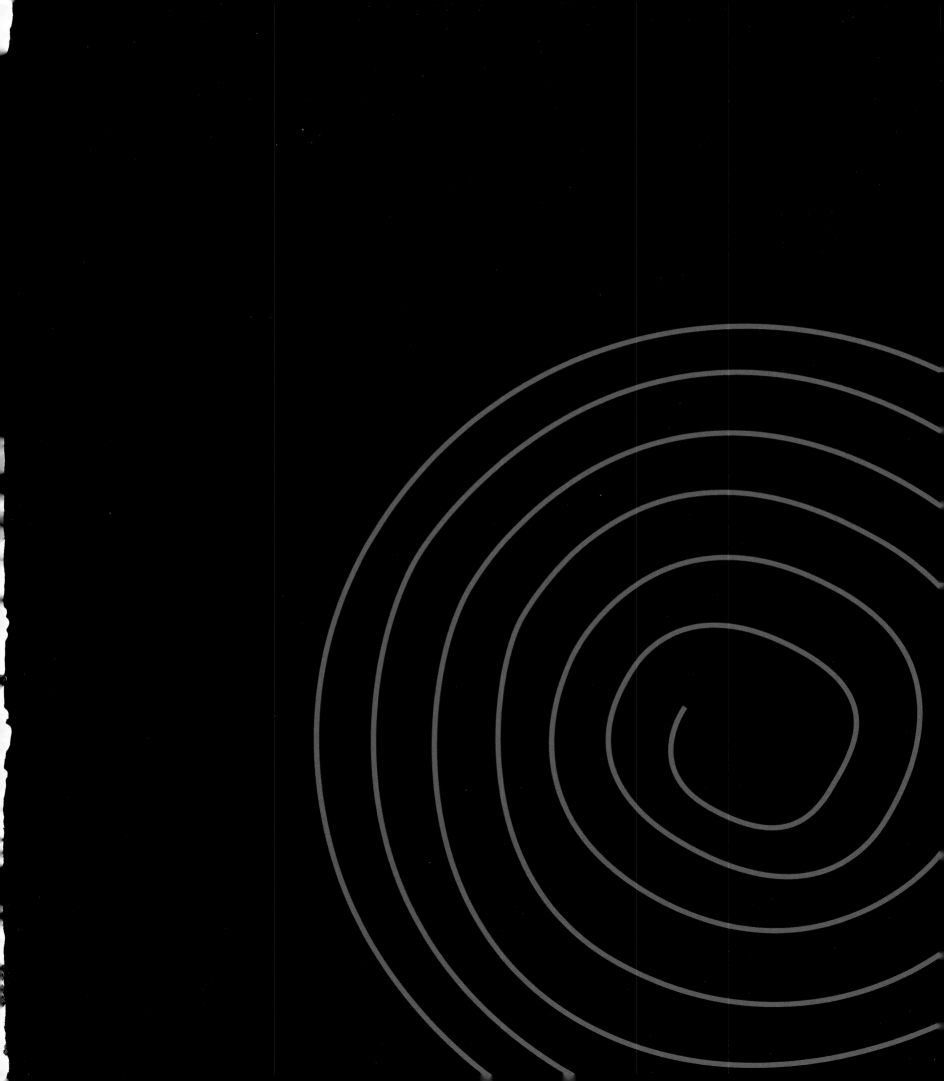

Legendary Rock Songs

WHITE STAR PUBLISHERS

Contents

Text by
NATHAN BRACKETT

project editor
Valeria Manferto De Fabianis
graphic design
Marinella Debernardi
editorial staff
Laura Accomazzo
editorial consulting and iconographic research
Marco De Fabianis Manferto

What makes a great song?

"The rock and roll 45 is the Darwinian peak of the species," Bono said in 2009. "It is by far the most difficult thing to pull off, and it's the very life force of rock and roll: vitality, succinctness and catchiness, whether it's the Sex Pistols, Nirvana, the Pixies, the Beatles, the Who, the Rolling Stones."

At one time there was nothing but the single: Popular musicians thought in terms of one song at a time; the single was the unit fans purchased, by which careers were measured. Look back at Chuck Berry's discography and it's hard to find any notable albums beyond the greatest hits collections. In the age of 78 rpm records, albums were literally collections of platters — each package contained a few discs, like a photo album. Then, as the apocryphal story goes (recreated in Bill Flanagan's "Evening's Empire"), record store owners realized they could get more money if they bundled one popular single in an album package with a few less-popular singles.

The modern music business was founded on this concept, as the 33 rpm long-player rose to prominence. Art followed commerce: beginning with Frank Sinatra's 50s albums, which were the first popular concept albums, and hitting a new level with the Beatles' "Sgt. Pepper's Lonely Hearts Club Band," the album was considered the highest possible achievement in rock and roll. The idea of the LP as a magnum opus peaked in the 70s, with bands such as Led Zeppelin (who made a show of not releasing any commercial singles) and bloated progressive rock bands such as Yes and Emerson,

Lake and Palmer. There were exceptions to this rule – for one, punk rock, which was driven by the energy of singles in the 70s. In the 80s and 90s, the single still ruled in genres like dance music and hip-hop, but for "serious" rockers, the album was king.

We are in a new age of the single. The Internet has destroyed the old music industry business model: customers can now buy songs they want for 99 cents in the iTunes store, without having to buy the songs they don't want — that is, if they're paying for music at all. And in the last decade, art has followed commerce back the other way: We live in a playlist culture, where bands can build a name on the Internet with a leaked song and a cool video. One of the most fun songs of 2010, Cee-Lo's "Fuck You," was a track you couldn't hear on the radio.

Pete Seeger once said, "All songwriters are links in a chain." The 80 songs in this book are proof of the single's staying power. This book is a tribute to the lasting power of rock and roll — and great songwriting — to change the times. In these pages are some of the greatest moments in popular music: Many of them, like Madonna's "Holiday," were first shots in what would be long careers. Others, like the Troggs' "Wild Thing," are practically one-hit wonders. Some are almost cliches ("Satisfaction"). The later songs – "Maps," by the Yeah Yeah Yeahs – aren't yet as ubiquitous as "Johnny B. Goode" or "Yesterday," but we think they will be some day.

Like many of the most important aspects of pop music, the format of early singles was determined by technology: The first records were made on cylinders designed by Thomas Alva Edison; then, in 1887, Emile Berliner patented the disc-shaped record. This flat record could be mass-produced, which gave rise to the record labels; the round platter would become the standard for the next 100 years. Singles arose at the end of the 19th century; at first, they were 10" in diameter and 78 rpm, mostly made out of brittle shellac. Songwriters couldn't write tunes longer than a few minutes because no more would fit on a record — hence the invention of the three-minute single. By 1955, the old 78 rpm disc had been edged out of the way by the smaller, crisper 45 rpm single, which was the format of choice for rock and rollers.

In the 1960s, technological breakthroughs finally allowed artists to fit more music on the single; when the Beatles recorded the seven-minute-long "Hey Jude," part of their inspiration was just to take advantage of the 45's new capacity. But if the concrete barriers to recording for longer than three minutes were gone, the imperative of the single — pop hooks, directness, energy — remained. "When rock music forgets about the 45, it tends toward progressive rock, which is like a mold that grows on old, burned-out artists who've run out of ideas," says Bono. "We have a soundtrack/Pink Floyd side of our band, and it has to be balanced by fine songwriting."

But what makes a great song? "A great song doesn't attempt to be anything," Jay-Z says. "It just is. When you hear a great song, you can think of where you were when you first heard it — the sounds, the smells. It takes the emotions of a moment and holds it for years to come."

Don't try to find a winning lyrical theme throughout these tracks. There are songs about steamboats and black magic women here; paranoid androids and wonderwalls. "It's nothing that can be reduced to a formula," said producer Rick Rubin. "It has more to do with how the song makes you feel. A great song takes you away, and usually hits at some larger universal truth — maybe one the writer isn't even aiming for necessarily."

Some of the great songwriters say it's all about provoking a reaction. Linda Perry, who wrote Christina Aguilera's "Beautiful" and many other hit songs, said, "When I put a great song on, I know I'm always going to have a reaction. This total stranger shows up in your life with this song, and you have an emotional attachment." Swedish producer Max Martin, the man behind many of Britney Spears' biggest hits, said, "A great song has that 'what the fuck?' factor — when you put it on, you react to it. A great song grabs your attention right away."

Jackson Browne takes the long view. "A great song speaks to you immediately," he said, "but over a period of years continues to speak to you. Usually it involves accessing some deeper mystery or issue that remains unresolved."

Kenny Gamble of the great Philly soul songwriting team of Gamble and Huff said it's all about giving people something they can relate to: "A great song talks about something that's true, that happens to everybody. When you hear a great song, you think it's about you." His partner, Leon Huff, said: "People don't remember a good story. But a great story, they remember that for a long time."

Technology is going to keep on changing music. For one thing, the digital revolution – and the widespread accessibility of cheap music making programs – has made it easier than ever for anyone to become a producer. Tracks made on basic programs such as Apple's GarageBand have made it onto the Top 40 (Usher's "Love in This Club" was actually recorded with the synth samples that come preloaded in the program.) "It's easier to make demos sound like finished, produced records," said Rubin, "which, in some cases, has made songwriters take a bigger role in the way final productions actually sound."

"Technology has caused the songwriting process to lose some of the magic," Jay-Z remarked. "A lot of times now, people working on a song aren't in the same room. Imagine if Michael Jackson and Quincy Jones hadn't been in the same room! Those records would have been totally different. I've had times when I changed one word because of something that somebody said in the studio and it changed the whole song."

And there's no substitute for a talented songwriter who is struck by inspiration. "Sometimes it was just things that caught our and attention," said Mike Stoller, one-half of the songwriting duo Leiber and Stoller. "Like with 'Yakety Yak', we were

in Jerry's apartment and he was in the kitchen making tea. I was playing this funny rhythm and he yelled," 'Take out the papers and the trash.' I yelled back one line about spending cash, and we had a song."

"When I'm writing a song that I know is going to work, it's a feeling of euphoria," said Jay-Z, "it's how a basketball player must feel when he starts hitting every shot, when you're in that zone." Kris Kristofferson had his own sports metaphor: "I don't golf," he said, "but I imagine it's like a good golf swing." Not all great lyrics come in a rush, though: "Sometimes it took me two weeks to finish one lyric," said great Motown songwriter Eddie Holland of the team Holland Dozier Holland. "After I was done, I didn't want to hear about it."

Songwriting for Paul Simon is a painful process of trial and error; a song can take him three months to finish. "I always feel that the situation is serious," he said. "I'm in a vacuum, it's a dearth, and then there's something – a few notes, a phrase – and I say, 'I guess there's something,' but it's so small that I don't even know whether to count it." Simon characterizes songwriting as a challenge, almost a test: "I realized [years ago] that what I was fascinated with, couldn't explain, was sound, that you can't really say why a combination of sounds is moving or feels really good and right – and the game was: Can I get the sounds on my head on tape?"

"With the best ones, like 'Me and Bobby McGee'," Kristofferson said, "it's kinda magical. They just come alive and become something separate from you. It's like one of your kids – you might have been responsible for starting it, but then you look and see it is its own creation."

Bob Dylan loves to throw up smokescreens about his process: "Songwriting? What do I know about songwriting? It tastes better out of a glass," he once said.

"For me it's always been more confessional than professional," he said in a more serious moment, "My songs aren't written on a schedule … Motivation is something you never know behind any song, really. Anybody's song, you never know what the motivation was. It's nice to be able to put yourself in an environment where you can completely accept all the unconscious stuff that comes to you from your inner workings of your mind. And block yourself off to where you can control it all, take it down. You have to be able to get the thoughts out of your mind."

"When you're writing one of those songs," said John Fogerty of Creedence Clearwater Revival, "your mind tunes into some ethereal radio station and allows you to hear what's coming through. When I was working on Proud Mary and I hit the chorus – 'rolling, rolling' – I just shook my head, and I knew it was an evolutionary leap for me."

Often the challenge is to know when to stop working on a song. "I spend a lot of time fighting myself to stay out of the way of a great song," said Jay-Z, "It's hard for me to leave a song alone, in its natural state. I want it to have that mass appeal, but once I start trying to push it too far, you can feel that something isn't right."

Perry sees some perils in the return to singles culture: "In the 90s," she said, "we sank back into the 50s, and it became all about the producer. We were finding people, throwing them into the studio, giving them a look, and suddenly they're selling millions of records and have a perfume out. I think we're coming out of that and going into the 60s – fuck that bullshit, people want to hear the cracks, the out-of-tune guitar. We're starting to raise the bar."

One crucial distinction for Perry: "The difference is that there were really great songs written in the 50s. Are people really going to listen to Britney Spears or "NSYNC 20 years from now? I don't think so."

That's okay as far as Bob Dylan is concerned. He doesn't care if any new songs get written: "The world don't need any more songs," he once said. "They've got enough. They've got way too many. If nobody wrote any songs from this day on, the world ain't gonna suffer for it. Nobody cares. There's enough songs for people to listen to, if they want to listen to songs. For every man, woman and child on Earth, they could be sent, probably, each of them, a hundred records, and never be repeated. There's enough songs. Unless someone's gonna come along with a pure heart and has something to say. That's a different story."

These eighty songs are some of the best parts of the story so far.

Rock Around the Clock • Hound Dog • Jailhouse Rock • Whole Lotta Shakin' Goin' On • Johnny B. Goode • Summertime Blues • What'd I Say • Surfin' USA • You Really Got Me • The House of the Rising Sun • My Generation • Yesterday • Like a Rolling Stone • I Heard it Through the Grapevine • Sympathy for the Devil • Born to be Wild • Living for the City • La Grange • Get Up, Stand Up • London Calling • Sultans of Swing • Highway to Hell • Knockin' on Heaven's Door • Sunshine of Your Love • Smoke on the Water • Hey Jude • Purple Haze • I'm Waiting for the Man • Somebody to Love • Light my Fire • Hey Joe • Wild Thing • California Dreamin' • Mr. Tambourine Man • Stairway to Heaven • Imagine • Tiny Dancer • Maggie May • Changes • Heart of Gold • School's Out • Catholic Girls • Sweet Child O' Mine • Heart of Glass • Comfortably Numb • Search and Destroy • Proud Mary • Whole Lotta Love • Black Magic Woman • The Sound of Silence • (I Can't Get No) Satisfaction • I Got You (I Feel Good) • Born to Run • Sweet Emotion • Paranoid • Me & Bobby McGee • Bohemian Rhapsody • Blitzkrieg Bop • Anarchy in the UK • We Will Rock You • Dancing Barefoot • When Doves Cry • Jump • Holiday • Pride and Joy • Billie Jean • Every Breath You Take • Under the Bridge • One • Wonderwall • Paranoid Android • Maps • Sweet Child O' Mine • 7 Nation Army • American Idiot • Fix You • Smells like Teen Spirit • Enter Sandman • Like a Prayer • Radio Free Europe • Respect

BILL HALEY
"Rock Around the Clock"

"Rock Around the Clock" was recorded by a veteran singer who was almost in his 30s, but for America and the world, it was an announcement from a new teenage nation: We are here and we have our own music. Haley started out as a country and western singer in the 1940s, with a journeyman band called the Saddlemen. Things didn't begin to take off for the group until they renamed themselves the Comets and began to cover R&B songs — first Ike Turner's "Rocket 88" (considered by many to be the first rock song ever), then a version of Big Joe Turner's "Shake Rattle and Roll," which became the first rock and roll song to hit the Top Ten.

"Rock Around the Clock" — written by Max C. Freedman and James E. Myers — was considered a disappointment at first; it barely dented the charts. But then, a year later, the producers of the movie "Blackboard Jungle" began looking for rock songs for the film's soundtrack. In an effort to see what teenagers were listening to, actor Glenn Ford borrowed some albums from his teenage son, Peter; one of them was "Rock Around the Clock." The song became an international sensation after the release of the film. It went on to become the first rock and roll record to hit #1 on the Billboard Pop charts; it would eventually sell 25 million copies. Most important, it marked a sea change in popular music. "I brought home Bill Haley's 'Rock Around the Clock' and the rest is history, as they say," said Marc Bolan of T. Rex. "It was the best thing I had ever heard."

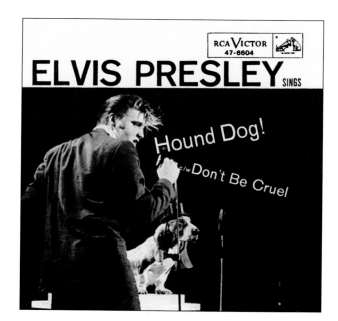

15 - Elvis on The Ed Sullivan Show in 1956; after his first, hugely successful appearance that year, Presley was invited back six weeks later.

1956

"Hound Dog" ELVIS PRESLEY

"Hound Dog" is the quintessential Elvis Presley song, and like Presley himself, "Hound Dog" spanned the differences between R&B, country and rock and roll. Originally written by the young Brooklyn songwriting duo Jerry Leiber and Mike Stoller, it was a hit for blues shouter Big Mama Thornton, who recorded a raunchy version in 1952. Almost half a dozen country and western versions were recorded shortly thereafter, by artists such as Eddie Hazelwood. Then Elvis heard a live version of the song by a lounge act at the Sands Hotel in Las Vegas called Freddie

Bell and the Bellboys; he liked the rhumba feel to the rhythm and asked his band to work up an arrangement. Elvis was meticulous during the recording process, making the band record 31 takes of the song before he was happy with the results.

Things caught fire after Presley performed the song on the "Milton Berle Show" in front of 40 million viewers. His electrifying, hip-shaking performance stoked a firestorm of controversy in the press (critics complained about his "caterwauling voice and nonsense lyrics" and gave Presley

the nickname "Elvis the Pelvis.")

The song became a huge hit, but songwriters Leiber and Stoller watched with mixed feelings. At first, Leiber says, they "heard the cash register ring," but at the same time they were disappointed that Presley changed the lyrics; Elvis had come up with the famous lines, "You ain't never caught a rabbit / And you ain't no friend of mine," all by himself. "To this day I have no idea what that rabbit business is all about," says Leiber. "Of course, the fact that it sold more than seven million copies took the sting out of that."

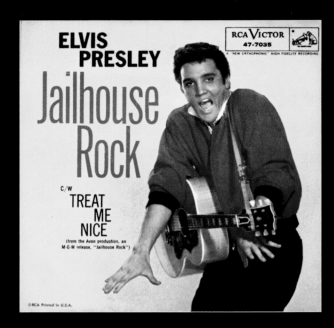

1957

ELVIS PRESLEY "Jailhouse Rock"

"Let's rock, everybody let's rock / Everybody in the whole cell block / Was dancing to the jailhouse rock." In 1957, rock and roll and juvenile deliquency seemed to go together in the mind of adult America, thanks in no small part to movies such as 1955's "Blackboard Jungle" (which helped launched Bill Haley's huge hit "Rock Around the Clock"). Elvis Presley's third movie, Jailhouse Rock, cashed in on that trend, featuring Elvis

starring as Vince Everett, a young man in prison who realizes he wants to be a professional rock and roll singer.

The centerpiece of the movie was one of Elvis' catchiest songs yet: "Jailhouse Rock," another winner by the songwriting team of Jerry Leiber and Mike Stoller. Perhaps still annoyed that Presley had departed from their lyrics on hits such as "Hound Dog," Leiber and Stoller worked some mischief into the lyrics

(the line "Number forty-seven said to number three / You're the cutest jailbird I ever did see" is a sly reference to prison sex). But what really sold the song was Elvis' powerful delivery and the swinging band. It opens with one of the most recogizable drum crashes in rock; drummer DJ Fontana said, "I tried to think of someone on a chain gang smashing rocks." The song was put over the top by the torrid Scotty Moore solo.

The performance of "Jailhouse Rock" in the film – a splashy production number featuring Elvis and a troupe of dancing inmates – would become one of rock's great cinematic moments. The single would become Presley's eighth #1 song, and marked the high point of the first part of Elvis' career. Just weeks after it fell from the charts, he received a draft notice from the U.S. Army. He would spend two years in the service.

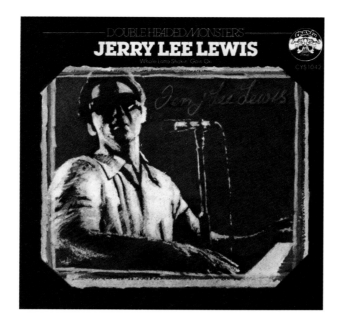

1957

JERRY LEE LEWIS

"Whole Lotta Shakin' Goin' On"

In October 1955, when Jerry Lee Lewis was still cutting his teeth playing the rough-and-tumble clubs around Natchez, Mississippi, a single arrived at the local radio station that he quite liked: "Whole Lotta Shakin' Goin' On" by Roy Hall.

"Jerry Lee liked the hell outta that damn record," said Lewis' bandleader at the time, Johnny Littlejohn. "He kept sayin',

'Lemme sing it.' I said, 'You don't know the words, Jerry Lee.' He said, 'Well, you can feed 'em to me.' And I fed 'em to him' and he sang the fire outta that sucker."

Two years later, Lewis had been signed by Sam Phillips Sun Records – also the home of Johnny Cash and Elvis Presley. The second song Lewis recorded was "Shakin'," which was by now a staple of his stage act. He

completely reworked Roy Hall's original version, adding locomotive piano and ad-libbed spoked vocals on the side. "I knew it was a hit when I cut it," said Lewis. "Sam Phillips thought it was gonna be too risqué, it couldn't make it. If that's risqué, I'm sorry."

In a sense, Phillips was right: Some radio stations would ban the song because of its

suggestive lyrics. But Lewis was more right: The song would reach #3 on the Billboard charts, #1 on the R&B charts and #1 on the country charts; Lewis would also deliver an incendiary performance on the Steve Allen television show, kicking his stool across the stage. As writer Nick Tosches would say: "Neither he nor Steve Allen had ever heard louder applause."

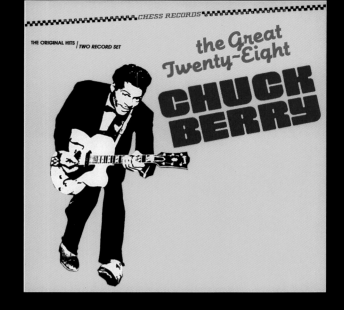

1958

CHUCK BERRY
"Johnny B. Goode"

You can hear rock and roll's roots loud and clear in Chuck Berry's greatest song: The famous guitar riff was an almost note-for-note copy of a lick from "Ain't That Just Like a Woman," a 1946 tune from jump blues king Louis Jordan. But more than anything, "Johnny B. Goode" pointed to the future: to the Beatles, the Rolling Stones and practically any band to feature an electric guitar as the dominant instrument over a 4/4 rhythm — that is, just about every rock band in existence.

"I used to absolutely slavishly copy Chuck Berry," Stones guitarist Keith Richards has said. "I practiced all the time." Brian Wilson and the Beach Boys were so taken with Berry that they copied his songs outright (converting Berry's "Sweet Little Sixteen" into their "Surfin' U.S.A." and "Johnny B. Goode" into "Fun Fun Fun") and sang his praises with lyrics like "Chuck Berry's gotta be the greatest thing that came along / He made the guitar beats and wrote the all-time greatest songs" (on "Do You Remember").

Berry originally intended "Johnny B. Goode" to be about his longtime piano player, Johnnie Johnson. (Johnson would stay out late partying after shows, and Berry would ask him "Why can't you just be good, Johnnie?") But it eventually became a song about Berry himself: he was the "little country boy" in the lyrics (the words were changed from "little colored boy," to make the song appeal to white America). The name "Goode" was taken from the street where Berry grew up in St. Louis. The genius of the song is that it can describe any aspiring rock guitarist; it has been covered as much as any song in rock history, by artists as diverse as the Sex Pistols, Jimi Hendrix and the Beatles. If you can't play "Johnny B. Goode," you can't play rock guitar.

Deep down in Louisiana
close to New Orleans
Way back up in the woods
among the evergreens
There stood a log cabin
made of earth and wood
Where lived a country boy
named Johnny B. Goode
Who never ever learned
to read or write so well
But he could play the guitar
just like a ringing a bell

1958

EDDIE COCHRAN "Summertime Blues"

"There had been a lot of songs about summer," said Eddie Cochran's manager and songwriting partner Jerry Capehart, "but none about the hardships of summer." Cochran and Capehart started with that concept, along with a blazing guitar riff Cochran adcreated, and ended up with "Summertime Blues"; it took them orty-five minutes to write.

Cochran was only 19 at the time, ut he already had an image as a ock and roll rebel; he wasn't as magnetic as Elvis Presley, but he had a tough, self-possessed cool. A handsome Minnesota teenager who played guitar, piano, bass and drums, Cochran had gotten his first break at the age of 18, when he performed the song "Twenty Flight Rock" in the Jayne Mansfield movie "The Girl Can't Help It." After that came the songs that established his legend: the chugging "C'mon Everybody," "Something Else" and "Summertime Blues."

Cochran had a huge effect on aspiring rockers: Paul McCartney actually played "Twenty Flight Rock" when he auditioned for the Beatles; George Harrison idolized Cochran, and he has been covered by artists as varied as the Beach Boys, Led Zeppelin, the White Stripes and the Sex Pistols. "Summertime Blues" has entered the charts a handful of times over the years: first in 1958 with Cochran, then ten years later with the hard rock band Blue Cheer's explosive version. The Who also covered "Summertime Blues" for their Live at Leeds album; it's one of their greatest, hardest live performances on record, and hit the charts in 1971.

Cochran's life was cut painfully short: during a tour of England in 1960, a taxi he was riding in with his girlfriend Sharon Sheeley and singer Gene Vincent hit a lamppost. Cochran was thrown through the windshield and died; he was 21.

29 - Ray Charles combined
gospel with R&B – and created
our modern idea of soul music

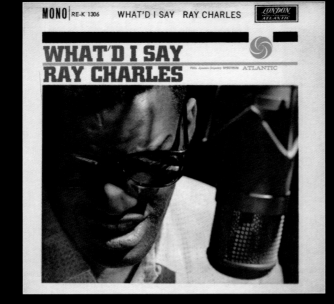

RAY CHARLES
"What'd I Say"

It was end of the night at a Ray Charles show in Brownsville, Pennsylvania; the year was 1958. Charles and his band had played every song they knew, but they were still obligated to play for another 12 minutes. So Charles told his back-up singers, The Raelettes: "Listen, I'm going to fool around, and y'all just follow me."

He started playing a deeply funky electric piano riff and improvising lyrics ("Hey Mama don't you treat me wrong / Come and love your daddy all night long / All right now / Hey hey / All

right"). The song climaxes with a riveting call and response between Charles and the Raelettes. "I'm not one to interpret my own songs, but if you can't figure out 'What I Say,' then something's wrong," Charles said later. "Either that, or you're not accustomed to the sweet sounds of love." The audience loved it so much that Charles called his producer and label boss, Jerry Wexler, and told him that he was going to record the song – which would become "What'd I Say" – as his next single.

It was his biggest single to

date, and the first to tear down the boundaries between R&B and gospel. The song's racy chants got it banned from many radio stations, but nothing would stop "What'd I Say." "Daringly different, wildly sexy, and fabulously danceable, the record riveted listeners," Charles' biographer Michael Lydon would write later. "When 'What'd I Say' came on the radio, some turned it off in disgust, but millions turned the volume up to blasting and sang 'Unnnh, unnnh, oooooh, oooooh' along with Ray and the Raelettes."

When you see me in misery
Come on baby, see about me
Now yeah, all right, all right,
aw play it, boy

When you see me in misery
Come on baby, see about me
Now yeah, hey hey, all right

See the girl with
the red dress on
She can do the Birdland
all night long
Yeah yeah, what'd I say, all right

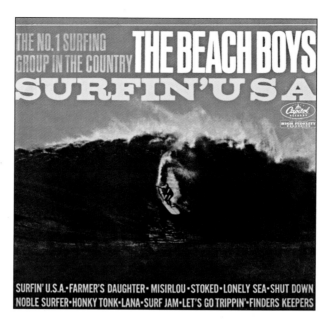

THE NO.1 SURFING GROUP IN THE COUNTRY **THE BEACH BOYS**
SURFIN'USA

SURFIN' U.S.A.•FARMER'S DAUGHTER•MISIRLOU•STOKED•LONELY SEA•SHUT DOWN
NOBLE SURFER•HONKY TONK•LANA•SURF JAM•LET'S GO TRIPPIN'•FINDERS KEEPERS

33 - Of all of the Beach Boys, only Dennis Wilson was a surfer; songwriter Brian had to rely on surfer friends for his info.

THE BEACH BOYS
"Surfin'USA"

Beach Boys songwriting mastermind Brian Wilson wasn't a surfer, but in 1963 he was dating a girl named Judy Bowles, and her brother, Jimmy, was a serious longboarder. Wilson was a fan of songs like Chubby Checker's "Twistin' U.S.A.," and Chuck Berry's "Sweet Little Sixteen," which tossed out the names of an array of cities. He had an idea: "I started humming the melody to 'Sweet Little Sixteen,' and I got fascinated with the fact of doing it, and I thought to myself, God! What about trying to put surf lyrics to 'Sweet Little Sixteen"s

melody?" He asked Jimmy Bowles to come up with a list of every surf spot he could think of. "And by God he didn't leave one out," Wilson said.

Brian recorded a demo of the song at home, with just him on piano, unaccompanied, before heading into the studio and letting Mike Love take the vocals to "Surfin'". The result was a rollicking rockabilly romp through sixteen surf spots — "Ventura County Line," "Doheny," Hawaii's "Waimea Bay," "Redondo Beach" — and the definitive song of the band's early career.

The song reached #3 on the Billboard charts — and came to the attention of Chuck Berry, who was not amused by the similarities to his "Sweet Little Sixteen." His lawyers approached Murry Wilson, Brian's father and the band's business manager; without consulting Brian, Murry gave Berry the sole songwriting credit, even for the lyrics Brian had written. Years later, Brian's brother Carl said the band ran into Berry in Denmark; Berry told them he loved the song — perhaps unsurprising, considering how much money it had made him.

45NP-5049

THE KINKS You really got me

IT'S ALL RIGHT

1964

THE KINKS
"You Really Got Me"

It's all about the riff: the bruising, perfectly distorted Dave Davies power chord that kicks off "You Really Got Me" and doesn't let up. It proved that a song could be built almost entirely around a killer guitar figure – that it could be the point of a song, not an adornment. This was a sentiment that would influence generations of hard rockers, from Pete Townshend (who has admitted that the Who's single "Can't Explain" was a copy of "You Really Got Me") all the way down to Metallica (who honored Kinks frontman Ray Davies by performing the song with him at the Rock and Roll Hall of Fame concerts in New York City in 2009).

"You Really Got Me" was originally a "jazz-type tune," according to Ray Davies, and the famous riff was played by a saxophone; that was the kind of music Davies recalled that he liked at the time. Then Dave played the riff on an amp speaker he had modified by driving needles into it and slashing it with "a Gillette single-sided blade." Years later, the song's place in the hard rock firmament would be confirmed by Van Halen, who recorded a blazing arena-rock cover version. But it was the original that fired the imaginations of a legion of garage rockers, punks and metal musicians. "I said I'd never write another song like it," Ray Davies said later. "And I haven't."

THE ANIMALS.
The house of the rising sun

1964

THE ANIMALS

"The House of the Rising Sun"

"'The House of the Rising Sun' is a song that I was just fated to," said Eric Burdon of the Animals. "It was made for me and I was made for it." The song had been around for about one hundred years before Burdon heard it; he came across folk-blues singer Josh White's version first, when he was a 10-year-old in the British city of Newcastle. The song originally recounted a woman's harrowing descent into prostitution in a New Orleans brothel.

But it was almost certainly Bob Dylan's version of the song – which made the protagonist a man and took away some of the sexual content – that inspired Burdon and his blues-rock band the Animals. The Animals were touring with Chuck Berry in England when they began playing an electrified version of "Sun." "It was a great song for the Chuck Berry tour because it was a way of reaching the audience without copying Chuck Berry," Burdon said. Response from crowds was so enthusiastic that the band decided to record the track.

"We did one take," said Animals drummer John Steel – with no overdubs, live in the studio. "[Producer Mickie] Most said, 'That's it, that's a single.'" Most said: "It only took fifteen minutes to make so I can't take much credit for the production. It was just a case of capturing the atmosphere in the studio."

Writer Dave Marsh called the tune "the first folk-rock song" – no one before had given a folk tune such a powerful electric boost. Despite being over four minutes

long – considerably longer than most singles on the radio at the time – "Sun" hit the #1 spot on both the U.S. and British charts. It knocked the Beatles off the top of the U.S. charts. The Beatles sent the Animals a note of congratulations. Dylan supposedly wasn't so happy when he heard it, but he was inspired. "The best aspect of it, I've been told, is that Bob Dylan, who was angry at first, turned into a rocker," Burdon said. "Dylan went electric in the shadow of 'The House of the Rising Sun.'"

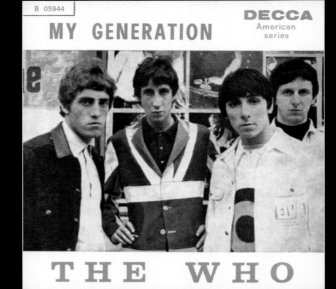

THE WHO
"My Generation"

When Pete Townshend wrote "My Generation," he had his fellow members of London's mod scene in mind, but it wasn't meant as a belligerent call to arms for Sixties youth. Instead, "Generation" was a statement of confusion, modeled after American jazz/blues man Mose Allison's "Young Man's Blues" ("Well the young man / ain't got nothing in the world these days"). "'My Generation' was very much about trying to find a place in society," Townshend told Rolling Stone in 1987. "I was very, very lost. The band was young then. It was believed that its career would be incredibly brief."

The Who tried all sorts of different arrangements for the song, fiddling with it for a month. At first it was considerably slower. It wasn't until they sped it up that it fell into place; the band ended up nailing the recording in two takes. Roger Daltrey's famous stutter ("why don't you all f-f-fade away") has been explained a couple of ways. One story is that the band's manager, Kit Lambert, told Daltrey that he should stutter like a speed addict. The other theory is simpler: that Daltrey needed help with the lyrics and was stumbling over the words. Whatever the case, it worked: "My Generation" would become the band's biggest hit in the United Kingdom. The Who's legend was sealed after a searing performance on the U.S. television show "The Smothers Brothers Comedy Hour," during which they destroyed their instruments. That wasn't unusual for the band at the time, but there was a mishap: at drummer Keith Moon's request, the stagehands overloaded Moon's drum kit with explosives. The resulting explosion damaged Pete Townshend's hearing permanently.

FINANCIAL TIMES
BRIERS
PRESENT
LAUGH
by NOËL COWARD
Directed by NIGEL PATRICK
RY
OMIC"
THE GUARDIAN

People try
to put us down
Just because
we get around
Things they do
look awful cold
I hope I die
before I get old

This is my generation
This is my generation, baby

THE BEATLES
YESTERDAY
ACT NATURALLY

5498
Capitol
RECORDS

1965

THE BEATLES "Yesterday"

Paul McCartney once called "Yesterday" "the most complete song I have ever written." But it took him eighteen months to record it. He had played it for producer George Martin (with the working title "Scrambled Eggs") but said that the band was "a little embarrassed by it. We were a rock and roll band." Another reason McCartney didn't record it immediately was that he wasn't sure he hadn't unconsciously lifted the melody from someone else – a testament to how universal and immediately accessible the tune is.

McCartney would record "Yesterday" with just George Martin and some hired string musicians. It was one of the first times a popular rock band used classical musicians on a track, and signified a new era for the band: a period when McCartney and Lennon would record their own separate songs under the Beatles name rather than writing songs together as they had for the early albums. "Yesterday" was also the first Beatles song that could not be reproduced at their shows without additional musicians. When they played it on "The Ed Sullivan Show," McCartney sang it with a backing track; at concerts, he would play it on acoustic guitar.

The Beatles would keep writing songs with more and more complicated arrangements, quitting the stage entirely after their 1966 tour. As for "Yesterday," it would go on to be the most covered song of all time, by artists from Frank Sinatra and Elvis Presley to Otis Redding and En Vogue. It also expanded the Beatles' appeal with older audiences. McCartney's partner Lennon admired the song from afar: "I have so much accolade for 'Yesterday,'" he said. "Beautiful – and I never wished I'd written it."

Yesterday
All my troubles
seemed so far away
Now it looks as
though they're
here to stay
Oh, I believe
in yesterday

Suddenly
I'm not half the man
I used to be
There's a shadow
hanging over me
Oh, yesterday came
suddenly

- Ringo Starr, Paul McCartney, George Harrison and John Lennon at Cliveden House in Buckinghamshire, England.

1965

BOB DYLAN
"Like a Rolling Stone"

"What a shocking thing to live in a world where there was Manfred Mann and the Supremes and Engelbert Humperdinck," said Elvis Costello, "and here comes 'Like a Rolling Stone'." "Like a Rolling Stone" was longer, meaner, louder, better than anything else on pop radio — and anything that Bob Dylan had written before then.

As captured in the documentary "Don't Look Back," Dylan was bored with his image as a folk musician in 1965 (you can see him working out the basic chords to "Rolling Stone" on the piano in the film, chords that he later said he took from "La Bamba" by Richie Valens.) "Like a Rolling Stone" was vengeful, electric, full of propulsion — the antithesis of the Sixties folk revival that had made Dylan its champion.

The lyrics spoke to a young woman who once "dressed so fine" but has fallen on hard times — has no more "secrets to reveal." You can read it as a cautionary tale or a spiteful rant, but it became a metaphor for a generation of middle-class youths who were walking away from "straight" society.

The music was just as liberated; the recording sessions were "totally disorganized, totally punk" remembers keyboard player Al Kooper. "It just happened."

Dylan was the ringmaster, though: he pushed blues expert Mike Bloomfield of the Paul Butterfield Blues Band out of his comfort zone and into something new and tough. "He said, 'I don't want you to play any of that BB King shit, none of that fucking blues. I want you to play something else'," recalls Bloomfield, who died in 1981.

The result was Dylan's biggest hit yet; listeners demanded that disc jockeys play the entire seven minutes, making it one of the longest singles ever to top the charts. But the song's real importance was in its truly liberated sprawl and raw energy. "It seemed to go on and on forever. It was just beautiful," said Paul McCartney, who listened to it with John Lennon at Lennon's home outside London. "He showed all of us that it was possible to go a little further."

You used to laugh about
Everybody that was hangin' out
Now you don't talk so loud
Now you don't seem so proud
About having to be scrounging
for your next meal

How does it feel
How does it feel
To be without a home
Like a complete unknown
Like a rolling stone?

48/49 - Bob Dylan in the studio;
from the beginning, he took an
often haphazard, intuitive
approach to recording music.

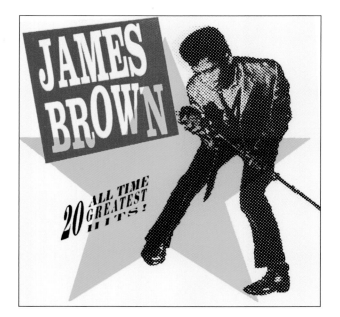

1965

JAMES BROWN
"I Got You (I Feel Good)"

James Brown wrote the basis of "I Got You" for his protégée Yvonne Faire: the original song was called "I Found You." "She did a good job on the song," said Brown, "right down to the holler. When I cut it myself, I just changed the lyric slightly."

What resulted was Brown's most instantly recogizable song: a pure-pop chorus and a ferocious groove, the latter powered by drummer Melvin Parker and his syncopated 16th note beats. The song got a big boost when Brown made a cameo on the Frankie Avalon teen film "Ski Party" in 1964, but because of record label feuding, Brown couldn't release the track as a record until eight months later. When "I Got You" was finally released, it powered to #3 on the Billboard pop singles chart. The single – along with the song that immediately proceeded it, "Papa's Got a Brand New Bag" – kicked off Brown's most successful stretch as a pop artist. He was constantly on the R&B charts for the next five years, touring all the time, and serving as a representative of the black community in meetings with politicians such as Vice President Hubert Humphrey. Brown's music would become even more rhythm-based on tracks such as "Cold Sweat" and "There Was a Time" – but "I Got You" was the template.

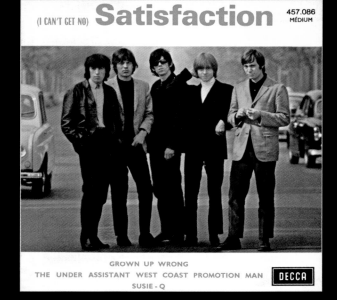

THE ROLLING STONES "(I Can't Get No) Satisfaction"

It is perhaps the greatest riff in rock: a fuzzed-out, piercing Keith Richards lick that jumps out of the radio every time you hear it. Richards came up with it in a dream one night, in a Florida motel room, during the Rolling Stones' third tour of America. "I was asleep," Richards told Rolling Stone. "I woke up in the middle of the night. There was a cassette player next to the bed and an acoustic guitar. I pushed 'record' and hit that riff for about a minute and a half, two minutes. Then I fell back to sleep. The next morning when I woke up, the tape had gone all the way to the end. So I ran it back, and there's like thirty seconds of the riff – Da-da da-da-da, I can't get no satisfaction – and the rest of the tape is me snoring!"

Richards played the riff and lyrical hook for Mick Jagger the next day; Jagger wrote the verses in ten minutes by the pool that same day. Jagger says: "It was my view of the world, my frustration with everything. Simple teenage aggression. It was about America, its advertising syndrome, the constant barrage." A few days later, the Stones went into the studio, where the guitars got their snarling fuzz treatment. "When it was by the pool," says Jagger, "it was a rather lilting acoustic melody. It only got to the snarl when we got this fuzz box in the studio, which was the first time we'd used one." The song was released two weeks later, and stayed at #1 on the U.S. charts for four weeks; it would be covered by everyone from Aretha Franklin to Devo. But most important, "Satisfaction" was a huge leap forward for rock: the Sixties had a new, hard, dangerous sound.

When I'm watchin' my TV
and a man comes on to tell me
how white my shirts can be
Well he can't be a man 'cause he doesn't smoke
the same cigarettes as me
I can't get no, oh no no no
Hey hey hey, that's what I say

54 - The Stones in Copenhagen, Denmark, 1965; "Satisfaction" was written on the road, beginning with a riff by Keith Richards.

55 - Mick Jagger's lyrics in "Satisfaction" were about being overwhelmed by advertising in America.

1965

SIMON AND GARFUNKEL
"The Sound of Silence"

Many people thought "The Sound of Silence" was about the Vietnam War; others, knowing that Paul Simon wrote it in the months after Nov. 22, 1963, thought it was about the assassination of President John F. Kennedy. In fact it was a plainspoken song about youthful alienation. When Simon sang the track's famous opening line, he was referring to a bathroom. "I used to go off in the bathroom," Simon said, "because it had tiles, so it was a slight echo chamber. I'd turn on the faucet so

that water would run — I like that sound, it's very soothing to me — and I'd play. In the dark." Hence: "Hello darkness, my old friend / I've come to talk with you again."

Folk duo Simon and Garfunkel had first recorded the song as an acoustic number, which appeared on the album Wednesday Morning 3 a.m. It flopped, and Simon and Garfunkel broke up, with Simon moving to England for a time. Then producer Tom Wilson, noticing the success of Bob Dylan's "Like a Rolling Stone,"

hired Dylan's backing band on that song to dub some electric parts over "Silence." It became a huge single, and Simon and Garfunkel reunited. "The key to 'The Sound of Silence' is the simplicity of the melody and the words," Simon said later. "It's a young lyric, but not bad for a 21-year-old. It's not a sophisticated thought, but it had some level of truth to it and it resonated with millions of people. Largely because it had a simple and singable melody."

ARETHA FRANKLIN
RESPECT

Respect
Dr. Feelgood
Think
Save Me

ATLANTIC
ATL 901

1965

"Respect" ARETHA FRANKLIN

When he performed live at the Monterey Pop festival in 1967, Otis Redding introduced "Respect" as the song "that little girl done stole from me." Redding had written it in 1965, about a man who was desperately trying to be acknowledged by his mate after a long day's work; it became a significant hit, reaching #5 on the R&B singles chart and #35 on the white pop charts. Then Jerry Wexler of Atlantic Records had the idea for his new artist – a gospel-trained soul singer named Aretha Franklin, whom he had recently brought over from Columbia Records – to record "Respect," thinking it would

be a nice showcase for Franklin's powerful voice. Wexler brought Franklin to Muscle Shoals, Alabama, to record with a group of all-white session musicians.

At first Aretha tried playing a faithful cover of the song on the piano; then things got more interesting when she and her sister Carolyn, who sang back-up vocals at the session, increased the tempo of the song. They also added some stomping call-and-response between Aretha and the other singers, which included the line "Sock it to me." "The fervor in Aretha's voice demanded that respect," Jerry Wexler wrote later,

"and more respect also involved sexual attention of the highest order. What else would 'sock it to me' mean?" Franklin and Wexler also added a new bridge, borrowed from the Sam and Dave track "When Something is Wrong with My Baby." Afterwards, Wexler called Redding and played him "Respect" over the phone; Redding knew then that he no longer owned the song.

"Respect" became one of the anthems of the burgeoning women's rights movement, and would far overshadow Redding's version, reaching #1 on the Billboard charts.

"Mr. Tambourine Man"

THE BYRDS

61 - The Byrds: Roger McGuinn, Chris Hillman, Mike Clarke, Gene Clark and Dave Crosby in Trafalgar Square, London.

Technically, "Mr. Tambourine Man" wasn't the first folk-rock song – see The Animals' "House of the Rising Sun" for that honor – but it was the song that truly melded the folk revival and rock and roll scenes, and popularized the new genre. Most of the Byrds were young folkies who were inspired by the Beatles to plug in their guitars: Roger McGuinn and Gene Clark both played in folk outfits with names like the New Christy Minstrels before meeting at the Troubadour club in Los Angeles. Next came David Crosby, who introduced Clark and McGuinn to A&R man Jim Dickson, and Chris Hillman. Dickson got them into the studio for demo tapes – "We were raw," admits Crosby – and eventually they were signed to Columbia Records.

"Dickson was the one that convinced us to sing Dylan songs," said Crosby. "He knew [Dylan] and got a test pressing of 'Tambourine Man' before it was out. We weren't sure about the song, but Jim got us to try it, and it worked." When time came to record the track, only McGuinn played on it, contributing his signature, chiming 12-string Rickenbacker guitar; Crosby and Clark also sang, but the rest of the instruments were played by session musicians hired by Dickson. "He didn't think we were strong enough to cut it," Crosby said. But that didn't spoil the excitement when the song became a hit: The band was driving along in an old '56 Ford station wagon when they first heard "Mr. Tambourine Man" on the radio. "We went crazy!" says Crosby. "We pulled over to the side of the road. It was just ecstasy."

1965

"California Dreamin'"

THE MAMAS AND THE PAPAS

63 · Pure pop happiness: The Mamas and the Papas in their Sixties prime.

Folk musician John Phillips was 28 years old, and his wife, Michelle, a slight, beautiful California native, was 19. They were newly married and had moved to New York City. "It was a very cold winter, and I hadn't been home to Los Angeles in so long, and I was so homesick," said Michelle. Then, one night, she continued, "John woke me up in the middle of the night and he said, 'Listen to the song I'm writing.' He sang, 'All the leaves are brown / And the sky is gray / I've been for a walk / On a winter's day.'"

Phillips hated writing by himself; he asked Michelle if she would write the rest of the song with him. "So I made myself get up – thank God! – and we wrote the song," Michelle said. The second verse ("Stopped into a church / I passed along the way / Well I got down on my knees / And I began to pray") recalled a visit Michelle had made a few days earlier to New York's St. Patrick's Cathedral. "I loved visiting churches," she said.

John and Michelle teamed up with singers Cass Elliott and Denny Doherty, and got an audition with record label executive Lou Adler. After they sang "California Dreamin'" and "Monday, Monday" in his office, Adler said, "I felt like, this must have been what George Martin felt when he discovered the Beatles." After letting folk musician Barry McGuire record "Dreamin'" with the Mamas and the Papas on backing vocals, Adler decided the song was too good to let go, and had the group record it for themselves. It wasn't a hit until it started to get a lot of airplay in Boston – appropriately enough, a city with a long, cold winter.

"1966"

THE TROGGS
"Wild Thing"

Andover, England group the Troggs (originally the Troglodytes) were looking for a break when their record label presented them with a choice of two songs to perform: John Sebastian's "Did You Ever Have to Make Up Your Mind?" and "Wild Thing" by 21-year-old Yonkers, New York-born songwriter Chip Taylor. "I looked at the lyrics – 'Wild thing ... you make my heart sing ... you make everything groovy,'" said singer Reg Presley, "and they seemed so corny that I thought, 'Oh God,

what are they doing to us?'" Even Taylor admitted the lyrics were silly; after recording his first demo of the song, the songwriter said, "I was on the floor laughing when I was through."

"Wild Thing" was recorded live in the studio, in two takes. It turned out to be the sound of pure hard rock perfection: a diabolically simple major-chord riff; a boatload of distortion; a bruising, straightforward lyric. Presley put it over the top with an almost comic ocarina solo in

the middle. It became the first hit single for the Troggs, reaching #2 in the United Kingdom and #1 in the United States. The band would never have another hit as big, but the influence of "Wild Thing" would grow as the years passed. It was famously covered by Jimi Hendrix at the Monterey Pop Festival, and would become a touchstone of garage rock and the punk and New Wave that followed. The lesson: never underestimate the power of sex and a great riff.

"HEY JOE"

JIMI HENDRIX

67 - Jimi Hendrix performing at the Hollywood Bowl; after kicking around as a sideman in the U.S. for years, Hendrix got his big break in the U.K.

The lyrics to "Hey Joe" sound like a traditional murder ballad, written by someone whose name has been lost to history: they follow a man who kills his girlfriend and flees to Mexico. The liner notes to Hendrix's album Are You Experienced? call it "a blues arrangement of an old cowboy song that's about 100 years old." An American songwriter named William Roberts is actually credited with writing "Joe" in 1962. By the mid-Sixties, it had become a trendy song on the rock scene; the Byrds, Love, the Standells and the Surfaris all logged versions. Many friends of Jimi Hendrix say he heard it from a folk musician named Tim Rose, but Hendrix's friend Curtis Knight says Jimi first heard a version by the California band the Leaves. "I was with Jimi when he bought the record, at a record store in New York," Knight says. "He always had some idea of what he wanted to do with that record."

Hendrix started playing "Hey Joe" with his band Jimmy James and the Blue Flames, playing venues such as Cafe Wha? in Greenwich Village. "It was his signature song," says musician Bob Kulick, who was on the scene as well. "There wasn't anybody around who could play like him."

1967

"Light My Fire"

THE DOORS

The first time Doors keyboardist Ray Manzarek heard guitarist Robbie Krieger play "Light My Fire," he said he thought it "was vaguely Sonny and Cher, sort of Mamas and Papas sounding, a jug band sort of song." It was one of the first songs Krieger had ever written; singer Jim Morrison had invited his band mates to try writing, and Krieger – inspired by Morrison's mythic, poetic songs – had attempted to pen lyrics with the themes of fire, earth, air and water. He settled on fire because he liked the Rolling Stones song "Play with Fire." Drummer John Densmore said the song "immediately sounded like a hit to me. It had a hook. It stuck in your memory the moment you heard it."

In the studio, the song ran an epic seven minutes long, with an extended keyboard solo from Manzarek and a guitar solo from Krieger; later they said they were inspired by John Coltrane's performance of "My Favorite Things" from "The Sound of Music," which also had an two solos in the middle of the song. "It was exactly what we were doing at the time at Whisky A Go Go," said Manzarek, referring to the famous home of their early club gigs, "letting the music take us wherever it might lead in a particular performance, just improvising." The Doors' record label edited the song down to less than three minutes when they released it as a single, thinking that it wouldn't be played on the radio otherwise.

Densmore was right: "Light My Fire" reached #1 on the Billboard singles chart, selling 1.2 million records, becoming the first chart topper for their label, Elektra Records, and launching the Doors' career.

70 - Jim Morrison of the
Doors performs at the
Kongresshalle in Frankfurt,
West Germany.

71 - Morrison at his famous
"young lion" photo session;
he would remain a sex symbol
years after his death in 1967.

jefferson airplane

JOURNEY ▶ the best of

featuring WHITE RABBIT • CROWN OF CREATION • SOMEBODY TO LOVE
BLUES FROM AN AIRPLANE • HAVE YOU SEEN THE SAUCERS • VOLUNTEERS

73 - At the heart of San Francisco's Haight-Ashbury scene: The Jefferson Airplane.

JEFFERSON AIRPLANE
"Somebody to Love"

"I had this friend in Berkeley who came up with funny names for people," Jorma Kaukonen said. "His name for me was Blind Thomas Jefferson Airplane (for blues pioneer Blind Lemon Jefferson). When the guys were looking for band names and nobody could come up with something, I remember saying, 'You want a silly band name? I got a silly band name for you!'" And so Jefferson Airplane was born. Founded by singer Marty Balin, the Airplane had kicked around the San Francisco psychedelic-folk scene for close to a year with singer Signe Anderson,

until she left to have a child. They found a replacement in Grace Slick, the singer for the Great Society, a band that opened for the Airplane occasionally. Slick was a gorgeous former model who had a ferocious voice that immediately raised the metabolism of the Airplane.

She also brought a couple of songs with her from her old group: "White Rabbit," an Alice in Wonderland-style song about taking pills, and "Somebody to Love," an aggressive song written by Great Society member Darby Slick (who was also Grace's brother-in-law). Darby said that

"Somebody" was about "doubt and disillusionment." The Airplane tore into the song during the sessions for their second album Surrealistic Pillow, under the auspices of "spiritual adviser" Jerry Garcia, transforming it from a sleepy folk-rock jam into a hard-rocking barn burner. "Somebody" reached #5 on the Billboard charts and put the new Haight Ashbury scene on the pop culture map; the Airplane would go on to perform it at Monterey Pop, as well as major network television shows such as The Smothers Brothers Comedy Hour and The Tonight Show with Johnny Carson.

When the truth is found to be lies
and all the joy within you dies
don't you want somebody to love
don't you need somebody to love
wouldn't you love somebody to love
you better find somebody to love

75 - Sixties-rock antiheroes:
The Velvet Underground threw
cold water on the hippie ideal.

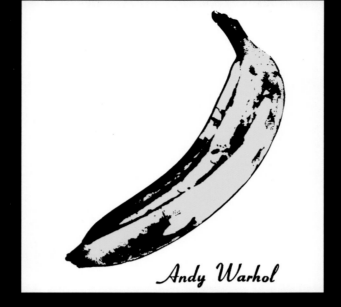

Andy Warhol

1967

THE VELVET UNDERGROUND
"I'm Waiting for the Man"

"Everything about that song holds true," Lou Reed said about "I'm Waiting for the Man," – "except the price." "Waiting" was the dark companion piece to Reed's drug opus "Heroin" on the Velvet Underground's debut album, The Velvet Underground and Nico. It captured in bleak, deadpan detail the story of a white man heading uptown to an apartment building at Lexington Avenue and 125th Street in Harlem to score 26 dollars' worth of heroin. "Waiting" started as a folkie acoustic song that Reed

wrote in the Lower East Side apartment he shared with John Cale. In the studio, the band gave it a propulsive electric strum plus a heavy dose of reverb and fuzz, which amped up the sense of desperation.

"Waiting for the Man" and "Heroin" scared many record labels away from the Velvets; Atlantic Records' Ahmet Ertegun wouldn't sign them unless they took the songs off the album. But inspired by the example of Andy Warhol – who took the VU under his wing for a time, and served as

nominal "producer" on their first album – the band insisted on keeping them, and signed with Verve. Warhol didn't actually help in the studio, but it didn't matter. "The advantage of having Andy Warhol as producer was that because he was Andy Warhol they left everything in its pure state," Reed said. "Right at the very beginning we discovered what it was like to be in the studio and record things our way, and have essentially total freedom."

"Waiting" was hardly a

commercial success when it was released, but it had an inordinate influence on those who heard it. Among them was a young David Bowie, who heard an early test pressing of the song. "I was in awe. It was serious and dangerous and I loved it," Bowie said. "I literally went into a band rehearsal the next day, put the album down and said, 'We're going to learn this song. It is unlike anything I've ever heard.' I must have been the first person in the world to cover a Velvet Underground song."

I'm waiting for my man/Twenty-six dollars in my hand/Up to Lexington, 125/Feel sick and dirty, more dead than alive/I'm waiting for my man/Hey, white boy, what you doin' uptown?/Hey, white boy, you chasin' our women

1967

"Purple Haze"

JIMI HENDRIX

It was the riff that announced the Summer of Love: an off-kilter, distorted tritone chord that has become shorthand for the psychedelic Sixties. Hendrix wrote the riff backstage at a London club gig; his manager Chas Chandler (also a member of the Animals) encouraged him to turn it into a song. Hendrix gave a different story practically every time someone asked him about the lyrics: "I dream a lot and I put a lot of my dreams down as songs," he once told New Musical Express. "'Purple Haze' was all about a dream I had that I was walking under the sea." He would also say that the song was inspired by his love of science fiction, a Hopi legend, and a guy who's so hung up on a girl that he's 'in a sort of daze.'" Of course, the song could just be about LSD, as many people thought at the time: the drug company Sandoz sold a version of the drug in purple pills that came to be called "purple haze."

Excitement around Hendrix was at a fever point in early 1967; practically the entire U.K. rock scene came to see the Experience play a show at the London club the Bag O' Nails: Paul McCartney, John Lennon and Ringo Starr of the Beatles; Eric Clapton; Pete Townshend; Jimmy Page; Jeff Beck; and Mick Jagger and Brian Jones of the Rolling Stones. Jones made a crack that in front of the stage "it was wet from all the guitar players crying."

Hendrix wrote a long early version of the lyrics called "Purple Haze – Jesus Saves," which was boiled down into the three minute version of the song that he and his band the Experience cut in January and February of 1967. The levels of distortion that the band used were so fierce that a note was enclosed to the U.S. label when it was sent overseas: "DELIBERATE DISTORTION: DO NOT CORRECT."

Purple haze all in my brain
lately things don't seem the same
Acting funny and I don't know why
excuse me while I kiss the sky

Purple haze all around
don't know if I'm going up or down
am I happy or in misery?
whatever at is a girl put a spell on me

80/81 - Jimi Hendrix
performs onstage at the
Monterey Pop Festival in 1967.

PURPLE HAZE

1968

THE BEATLES "Hey Jude"

Who is the "Jude" in Paul McCartney's 1968 masterpiece? John Lennon thought McCartney was singing to him; the Beatles were going through a difficult time, and Lennon believed "Hey Jude" was McCartney's way to say goodbye. "Yoko's just come into the picture," said John.

"Subconsciously, he was saying, Go ahead, leave me." Judith Simons, a journalist with the Daily Express, believed McCartney was singing about her. When Lennon asked him, McCartney said he was singing to himself.

In fact, "Jude" was Julian Lennon, John Lennon's then-5-year-old son, to whom McCartney was close. McCartney wrote the basic song in his car, on his way to visit Julian and his mother Cynthia Lennon, whom John had left for Ono. "Paul and I used to hang out quite a bit," Julian said. "There seems to be far more pictures of me and Paul playing together at that age than there are pictures of me and my dad." The song was "a hopeful message to Julian," said

McCartney. "'Come on, man, your parents got divorced. I know you're not happy, but you'll be OK.'" It was originally going to be called "Hey Jules," but McCartney said, "I changed it to 'Hey Jude' because I thought that sounded a bit better."

The result was one of the Beatles' most affecting, emotional songs – amplified by the prolonged, sing-along chorus at the end. The band hired a 40-piece orchestra for the sessions; the classical musicians were

asked to sing and clap along, for double their usual fee. Everyone complied, except for one: "I remember one bloke saying he wasn't going to clap hands and he wasn't going to sing," said producer George Martin. "He said his union card said he was a violinist, and he walked out of the studio. Much to everybody's amazement."

"Hey Jude" ended up being the Beatles' longest song –7 minutes, 11 seconds – and their biggest hit up to that point.

Hey Jude don't make it bad,
take a sad song and make it better,
Remember to let her into your heart.
then you can start to make it better.

Hey Jude don't be afraid
You were made to go out and get her,
the minute you let her under your skin
Then you'll begin to make it better.

And any time you feel the pain
hey Jude refrain don't carry the world upon
                              your shoulders

For well you know that's it, a fool who plays it cool
by making his (life/world) a little colder.

Hey Jude, don't let me down.
She had found you now make it better
Remember to let her into your heart,
then you can start to make it better.

So let it out and let it in, hey Jude begin
You waiting for someone to perform with
& dont you know that it's just you

CREAM
"Sunshine of Your Love"

Atlantic Records chief Ahmet Ertegun, who was presiding over the recording sessions for Cream's Disraeli Gears album, thought "Sunshine of Your Love" was "psychedelic hogwash." Bassist/singer Jack Bruce had come up with the song with his friend, beat poet Pete Brown, during an all-night recording session; the sky was turning light when Brown came up with the line "It's getting near dawn / When lights close their tired eyes." Bruce's bass line – one of the great riffs in hard rock – was inspired by Jimi Hendrix, whom Bruce and Eric Clapton

went to see perform that year.

Luckily, Ertegun turned control of the Disraeli Gears session over to producer Felix Pappalardi, who was more open to the song, and the atmosphere in the studio became looser. But "Sunshine" didn't come together easily. "There just wasn't this common ground that they had on so many of the other songs," said engineer Tom Dowd. "I said, 'Have you ever seen an American Western where the Indian beat – the downbeat – is the beat? Why don't you play that one?' [Drummer] Ginger [Baker] went inside and they started to run the song again. When they started

playing that way, all of the parts came together and they were elated." Clapton delivered a monster guitar solo which made reference to the standard "Blue Moon"; the idea was to balance the sun in the song with the moon.

Still, Atlantic Records wasn't convinced by the song, and was going to reject it. Then, Bruce says, "Booker T. Jones and Otis Redding heard it and told me it was going to be a smash." It was released, and now you can hear it in any music store on any day of the week: it's the first song most prospective buyers play on a new guitar.

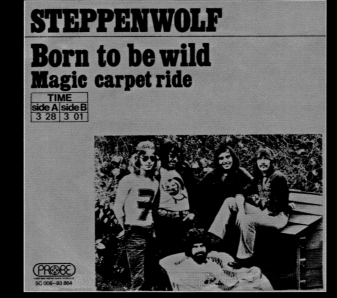

STEPPENWOLF
"Born to be Wild"

"Born to be Wild" will perhaps always be associated with actors Dennis Hopper and Peter Fonda blazing down an open highway on Harley Davidson motorcycles. It's easily the greatest biker song of all time, synonymous with pure freedom. "Every generation thinks they're born to be wild," said Steppenwolf singer John Kay, "and they can identify with ['Born'] as their anthem."

It was written by Mars Bonfire (born Dennis McCrohan), the brother of Steppenwolf's drummer. "I was walking down Hollywood Boulevard one day," Bonfire recalls, "and saw a poster in a window saying 'Born to Ride' with a picture of a motorcycle erupting out of the earth like a volcano with all this fire around it. Around this time I had just purchased my first car, a little secondhand Ford Falcon. So all this came together lyrically: the idea of the motorcycle coming out along with the freedom and joy I felt in having my first car and being able to drive myself around whenever I wanted."

Steppenwolf, fronted by growling John Kay, worked up the arrangement to the song in twenty minutes in the studio. "Everybody [was] playing just what they felt like playing," drummer Jerry Edmonton says. Like many of the band's songs, it ends with a simple fade-out. The reason: "Because we were set up so we couldn't see each other, we'd have sloppy endings," says Edmonton. At first, "Born to be Wild" was just a placeholder on the Easy Rider soundtrack; Peter Fonda wanted Crosby, Stills and Nash to do the music for the film. The song ended up staying. Its other claim to fame: Bonfire's lyric "heavy metal thunder" was the first time the term had been used in a rock song; it would give a new genre its name.

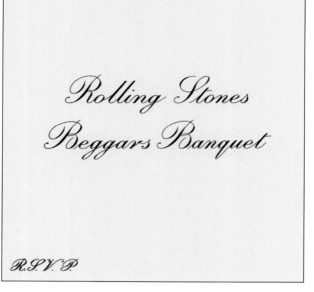

1968

Rolling Stones
Beggars Banquet

R.S.V.P.

THE ROLLING STONES
"Sympathy for the Devil"

Keith Richards says that "Sympathy for the Devil" was just the band giving the media what they thought they already saw. He told Rolling Stone magazine: "Before, [when] we were just innocent kids out for a good time, they're saying, 'They're evil, they're evil.' Oh, I'm evil, really? So that makes you start thinking about evil. Everybody's Lucifer."

Mick Jagger credits the poet Charles Baudelaire for inspiring "Sympathy:" "It was an idea I got from French writing," Jagger said, "and I just took a couple of lines and expanded on it. I wrote it as sort of like a Bob Dylan song." But he was obviously influenced by Mikhail Bulgakov's novel "The Master and Margarita," which features the devil as an upper-class character in the 1930s; Marianne Faithfull had given it to Jagger as a present.

According to Richards, he wasn't sure how to arrange the song, as a folk song or a samba. The samba won, fortunately; conga player Rocky Dijon laid down a mesmerizing rhythm, and Charlie Watts play what he called a Kenny Clarke-style drumbeat. "'Sympathy' was one of those sort of songs where we tried everything," said Watts.

'It has a very hypnotic groove, which has a tremendous hypnotic power, rather like good dance music," Jagger said. "It doesn't speed up or down. It becomes less pretentious because it's a very unpretentious groove. If it had been done as a ballad, it wouldn't have been as good."

Please allow me to introduce myself/I'm a man of wealth and taste/ I've been around for a long, long year/Stole many a man's soul and faith/

90 - The Rolling Stones recording "Sympathy For the Devil"; director Jean-Luc Godard was filming.

91 - The Rolling Stones in 1968: Charlie Watts, Brian Jones with sitar, Bill Wyman.

I was 'round when Jesus Christ/Had his moment of doubt and pain/ Made damn sure that Pilate/Washed his hands and sealed his fate

MARVIN GAYE
I HEARD IT THROUGH THE GRAPEVINE

THE ORIGINAL VERSION OF THE SONG FEATURED IN THE **501** COMMERCIAL

1968

MARVIN GAYE
"I Heard it Through the Grapevine"

Motown Records chief Berry Gordy hated "I Heard it Through the Grapevine" the first time he heard it. Staff writers Norman Whitfield and Barrett Strong had come up with the tune, and Smokey Robinson and the Miracles cut the first version, an up-tempo arrangement with a classic big Motown beat. It was played at the regular Motown quality control meeting. Gordy thought it was horrible and refused to release the single. But the stubborn Strong and Whitfield believed in their song,

and rerecorded it as a down-tempo, sultry number, with string accents and a magnificent vocal performance by Marvin Gaye.

Whitfield loved to record his songs in a number of different contexts, until he hit on something that worked. A young group called Gladys Knight and the Pips was also looking for material – specifically something to "out-funk" Aretha Franklin, who was having a run of hits with songs like "Respect" and "Think." So Whitfield adapted "Grapevine" into

a stomping rave-up for them; the Pips version was released before Gaye's, and became a significant hit, reaching #1 on the Billboard R&B charts and #2 on the pop charts. It was Motown's biggest hit up to that point, but Whitfield believed Gaye's version could be even bigger. He was right; Gordy agreed to put it out after refusing at first, and Gaye's performance reached the top of the pop charts, staying there for seven weeks; it would become Motown's biggest hit of the decade.

1969

CREEDENCE CLEARWATER REVIVAL *"Proud Mary"*

As a songwriter, John Fogerty of Creedence Clearwater Revival drew on the blues, gospel, country and New Orleans R&B – and he also knew how to write a hit. He kept a notebook of song ideas with him, including titles, which he considered crucially important to songs' success. "When it came to songwriting," Fogerty once said, "I learned that the title must be important. If you have a cool title like 'Ramrod' or 'Heartbreak Hotel' or 'Bad Moon Risin' on top of everything else, you're really

setting off in the right direction."

At the front of Fogerty's notebook of ideas was the title "Proud Mary." At first, "I pictured [the song] being about a maid in a household of rich people," Fogerty said. "She gets off the bus every morning and goes to work and holds their lives together. Then she goes home." Fogerty also got the idea to make the song about a Mississippi riverboat, after seeing one on the Western television show Maverick. Fogerty was watching with a friend who said,

"Hey, riverboat, blow your bell." Fogerty thought: "Yeah, that might be part of it, too."

Creedence Clearwater Revival had had a hit with "Suzie Q." already, but their next single, "I Put a Spell on You," had dropped off the charts after a short while. The pressure was on for another successful song. Fogerty was also still enlisted in the Army Reserves, which was a drain on his time and energy.

Then one day he got a letter in the mail saying he had been

honorably discharged from the military. "I was so happy, I ran out onto my little patch of lawn and turned cartwheels," Fogerty said. "Then I went into my house, picked up my guitar, and started strumming. 'Left a good job in the city.' And then several good lines came out of me immediately ... By the time I hit 'Rolling, rolling, rolling on the river,' I knew I had written my best song." He had: "Proud Mary" hit #2 on the charts – the first of five songs in a row from CCR to do so.

1969

LED ZEPPELIN
"Whole Lotta Love"

It's one of the mightiest guitar riffs in rock – coupled with the definitive howling Robert Plant vocal: "You need coolin', / Mama I ain't foolin', / I'm gonna send you / back to schoolin.'"

"['Whole Lotta Love'] was put together when we were rehearsing some music for the second album," says Jimmy Page. "I had a riff, everyone was at my house, and we kicked it from there."

"Page's riff was Page's riff," Plant says. "It was there before anything else. I just thought,

'well, what am I going to sing?'" He ended up riffing on American songwriter Willie Dixon's "You Need Love," which had been recorded by Muddy Waters a few years earlier, using some of the most memorable phrases: "Way down inside / Woman you need love." An even bigger influence was "You Need Loving," a raucous interpolation of Dixon's song by the U.K. band the Small Faces featuring blues singer Steve Marriott. Plant idolized Marriott: "I could never be compared with Steve Marriott because he's too

good, unfortunately!" Plant said later, "He's got the best white voice, for sheer bravado and balls."

The song featured a spaced out breakdown in the middle, which producer Eddie Kramer called "a combination of Jimmy and myself just flying around on a small console twiddling every knob known to man." Plant's ghostly vocals during the breakdown were an accident, Kramer explains: "At one point there was bleed-through of a previously recorded vocal ... It was the

middle part where Robert screams "Wo-man. You need it." Since we couldn't re-record at that point, I just threw some echo on it to see how it would sound and Jimmy said "Great! Just leave it."

Radio programmers couldn't get enough of "Whole Lotta Love," although many of them edited out much of that middle section by hand. Seven years later, Willie Dixon sued the band for songwriting credit, and was paid a settlement. Plant admits that the lyrics were "a nick. Now happily paid for."

98 - Led Zeppelin are almost as legendary for their bacchanalian backstage exploits as they are for their music.

99 - Jimmy Page liked to wheel out a squealing instrument called a theremin during shows, which he would control with hand movements.

You need coolin', baby, I'm not foolin', I'm gonna send you back to schoolin', Way down inside honey, you need it,

100 - The original golden god, as immortalized by the movie "Almost Famous:" Robert Plant.

101 - When drummer John Bonham died, Led Zeppelin could not continue; he was the band's secret ingredient.

I'm gonna give you my love, I'm gonna give you my love.
Wanna whole lotta love /Wanna whole lotta love

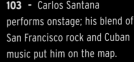

1970

SANTANA
Black Magic Woman"

Carlos Santana's father was a mariachi player in Mexico, where Carlos was born. "I joined my father in the streets, playing boleros," Santana told Rolling Stone. "But I had my ear on Chuck Berry, Little Richard and Bo Diddley." Later, as a teenager in San Francisco, Santana would go to the Fillmore to hear artists like Jeff Beck, Jimmy Page, B.B. King and U.K. bluesman Peter Green of Fleetwood Mac. Santana's great innovation was to, as he put it, "integrate Tito Puente, Afro-Cuban musicians like Mongo Santamaria, into

the blues that I loved."

"Black Magic Woman" was where most of the world first heard that combination. It's a song that has become so well associated with Santana that few people realize it was a cover of a Green original; Santana's version, sung by keyboardist Gregg Rolie (later of the band Journey) stayed faithful to the spirit of Green's song, but opened it up with a blazing, Latin-funk introduction, then lurched into a cover of the jazz standard "Gypsy Queen" at the end.

Santana's band was a favorite

at the Fillmore as well, but had their debut to a broader rock audience at the Woodstock festival. "It was beyond scary," says Santana of playing the festival, "because I was at the peak of acid. I said, 'Please God, help me stay in tune. I promise I'll never touch this stuff again.'" Santana laughs: "Of course, I lied."

They made it through the gig, and the rock world was listening. "Within a year, everybody had conga and timbales: The Rolling Stones, Sly Stone, Jimi Hendrix, Miles Davis," Santana says.

1970

"Paranoid"

105 - Black Sabbath: Their name was taken from the occult fiction of author Dennis Wheatley.

BLACK SABBATH

"People feel evil things," Black Sabbath bassist Geezer Butler told Rolling Stone in 1971, "but no one ever sings about what's frightening and evil. I mean the world is in a right fucking shambles." Lead singer Ozzy Osbourne added: "There's a lot of paranoia going around." Black Sabbath caught the (still relatively young) rock establishment by surprise when they first hit big in 1971. They appealed to 15- and 16-year-old boys who were looking for something harder and heavier than the Beatles and the Rolling Stones, and got more than their share of condescension from rock critics and radio programmers.

"Paranoid" was a mission statement of sorts for what would become heavy metal: chugging, brutally simple power chords from guitarist Tony Iommi, and high-octane howls from Osbourne ("Finished with my woman 'cause she couldn't help me with my mind / People think I'm insane because I am frowning all the time"). Iommi came up with the basis of "Paranoid" in Regents Studio while the other band members were at lunch. "I started fiddling about with the guitar and came up with this riff," he recalled. "When the others came back, we recorded it on the spot."

It's impossible to overstate the influence that Sabbath had on future generations of metal musicians. "All the compelling themes are on Black Sabbath's records: beauty, atrocity, the seven deadly sins," said guitarist Dave Navarro. "Their music can make you think of walking on the beach with your wife, or of locking yourself in your room with your big toe on the trigger of a shotgun – sometimes within the same song."

Finished with my woman 'cause she couldn't help me with my mind/People think I'm insane because I am frowning all the time/All day long I think of things but nothing seems to satisfy/Think I'll lose my mind if I don't find something to pacify

I need someone to show me the things in life that I can't find
I can't see the things that make true happiness, I must be blind
Make a joke and I will sigh and you will laugh and I will cry
Happiness I cannot feel and love to me is so unreal
And so as you hear these words telling you now of my state
I tell you to enjoy life I wish I could but it's too late

106 - Sabbath's Geezer Butler, Ian Gillian and Tony Iommi; Iommi lost the tips of his fingers in a workplace accident.

107 - Ozzy Osbourne in concert; later in life he would become a reality television star with his family on MTV.

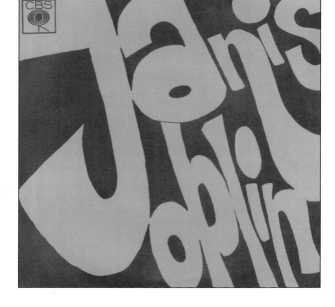

109 - Janis Joplin: Her mother described her as an "unhappy and unsatisfied" youth in Texas.

JANIS JOPLIN
"Me & Bobby McGee"

Songwriter Kris Kristofferson had a brief fling with Janis Joplin, and was a drinking chum as well. But he didn't write "Me & Bobby McGee" for her. The song came from when he was a struggling songwriter still making ends meet as a helicopter pilot. Fred Foster, the head of his record label, called to say he had a song title for him: "Me and Bobbie McKee" – named after Foster's secretary. Kristofferson misheard it as "Bobbie McGee."

"I thought there was no way I could ever write that," he said, "and it took me months hiding from him, because I can't write on assignment. But it must have stuck in the back of my head."

Kristofferson based the story of "Bobbie McGee" on Federico Fellini's La Strada: "I developed this story of these guys who went around the country kind of like Anthony Quinn and Giulietta Masina in La Strada," Kristofferson explained. "At one point, like he

did, he drove off and left her there. That was 'Somewhere near Salinas, I let her slip away.' Later in the film, he goes out, gets drunk, gets into a fight in a bar and ends up on the beach, howling at the stars. And that was where 'Freedom's just another word for nothing left to lose' came from, because he was free from her, and I guess he would have traded all his tomorrows for another day with her."

Joplin recorded "McGee" three

days before she died. It was a stunning example of her growth as an artist. She had been more or less a blues belter before; now she was a mature singer who could turn a country weeper into something bold and powerful. Kristofferson didn't know Joplin had recorded "McGee" until after she died; it would go on to become her first #1 single, and – after Otis Redding's "Dock of the Bay" – one of the very few posthumous #1 hits in rock history.

I pulled my harpoon out of my dirty red bandanna,
I was playing soft while Bobby sang the blues.
Windshield wipers slapping time, I was holding Bobby's hand in mine,
We sang every song that driver knew.

110 - As a teenager, Joplin listened to the music of Odetta and Big Mama Thornton.

111 - Joplin's college newspaper profiled her in 1962 with an article titled "She Dares to Be Different."

LED ZEPPELIN
"Stairway to Heaven"

According to Jimmy Page, "'Stairway to Heaven' crystallized the essence of [Led Zeppelin]. It had everything there and showed us at our best." Almost forty years after it was recorded, "Stairway" is still rock and roll's most famous mini-suite: an epic eight minutes that builds from a folkie, Elizabethan opening to a huge electric crescendo. Along with Queen's "Bohemian Rhapsody" and the Who's "Tommy," "Stairway" is the ultimate marriage of rock power and classical ambition.

Shortly after Led Zeppelin's fifth American tour ended, Jimmy Page and Robert Plant were staying at Bron-Yr-Aur, a cottage in the Welsh mountains where they would sometimes go to relax. It was there that Page came up with the beginnings of the guitar parts to "Stairway." "I had these pieces, these guitar pieces, that I wanted to put together," he recalls. "I had a whole idea of a piece of music that I really wanted to try and present to everybody."

"Page and Plant would come back from the Welsh mountains with the guitar intro and verse," recalled John Paul Jones. "I literally heard it in front of a roaring fire in a country manor house!"

Plant wrote most of the lyrics to the song in one evening, at Headley Grange, the mansion where they would sometimes work in Hampshire. He says it felt as if the lyrics were writing themselves: "My hand was writing out the words, 'There's a lady who's sure, all that glitters is gold, and she's buying a stairway to heaven'," Plant said. "I just sat there and looked at them and almost leapt out of my seat." The lyrics deal with a woman who's caught up with material acquisition, and are heavily informed by Plant's love of Celtic mythology and the work of J.R.R. Tolkien.

The song was an enormous hit when it was released, despite the fact that it was eight minutes long – almost three times the length of the average radio single. Conspiracy theorists suspected that the record had some sort of satanic message if you played the song backwards. Plant quashes this idea: "'Stairway To Heaven' was written with every best intention, and as far as reversing tapes and putting messages on the end, that's not my idea of making music."

To this day, "Stairway" is played thousands of times a year on classic rock radio. "It was a milestone," said Page. "Every musician wants to do something of lasting quality, something which will hold up for a long time. We did it with 'Stairway'."

There's a lady who's sure
all that glitters is gold
And she's buying a
stairway to heaven
When she gets there
she knows, if the stores
are all closed
With a word she can get
what she came for
Ooh, ooh, and she's buying
a stairway to heaven

1971

"IMAGINE"

JOHN LENNON

117 - John Lennon onstage at the Chrysler Arena in Ann Arbor, Michigan, on Dec. 10, 1971.

"Imagine" is as simple as a children's song, with a message – "Imagine there's no countries / And no religion too" – that John Lennon said was right out of The Communist Manifesto. Lennon called his Imagine album "Plastic Ono with chocolate coating." He was coming off the critical success of his soul-baring album Plastic Ono Band, which contained brutally personal songs such as "Mother," "God" and "Working Class Hero." Sales for Ono were respectable but not great; Lennon thought he could do better without compromising his message. He was particularly disappointed that the song "God," one of his favorites, didn't have the impact he wished.

"Imagine" was his attempt to aim higher. He composed it in his bedroom at his Tittenhurst Park estate, in Ascot, England, on the white grand piano that was featured in many of his videos. Yoko Ono says "Imagine" is "just what John believed: that we are all one country, one world, one people. He wanted to get that idea out." Lennon admitted that the idea for "Imagine" came from Ono: "The song was originally inspired by Yoko's book 'Grapefruit,'" he said. "In it are a lot of pieces saying, 'Imagine this, imagine that.' Yoko actually helped a lot with the lyrics, but I wasn't man enough to let her have credit for it."

Lennon's "chocolate coating" succeeded; "Imagine" only hit #3 on the singles charts when it was released, but over time it became his most commercially successful, most covered solo work. And to this day, you can hear children sing "Imagine" at school assemblies.

1971

"ELTON JOHN" "Tiny Dancer"

The "seamstress for the band" named in "Tiny Dancer" truly did exist; Elton John's partner, lyricist Bernie Taupin, wrote the song for his first wife, Maxine Feibelman. (Taupin has also said that the song was meant to capture the essence of California in 1970, and the spirit of women who traveled with rock bands in general.) "Dancer" fit in the framework of Madman Across the Water, an album full of downtrodden heroes such as "Levon" and the mentally ill protagonist of the title track.

"Tiny Dancer" ended up being a six-minute-plus major production, moving from pedal steel guitar to a big orchestral finish. Arranger Paul Buckmaster was brought in for the strings at the end of the song; Rick Wakeman, later of the band Yes, played keyboards. Despite the length – and the fact that it had a slow start as a single, peaking at only #41 on the Billboard charts – "Dancer" would become one of the John's most popular songs. It enjoyed a second life thanks to former Rolling Stone reporter Cameron Crowe's hit movie "Almost Famous," and has been covered by artists as diverse as Ben Folds and country star Tim McGraw.

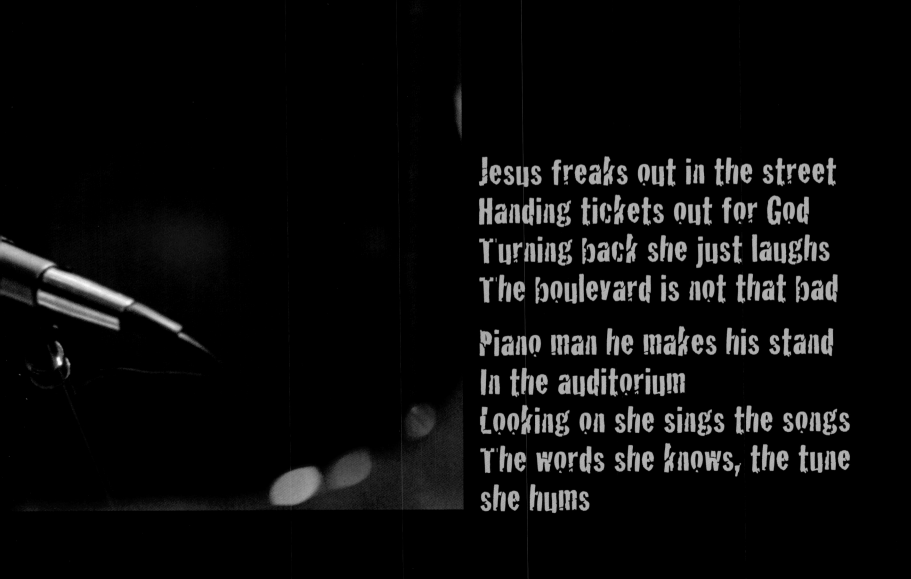

Jesus freaks out in the street
Handing tickets out for God
Turning back she just laughs
The boulevard is not that bad

Piano man he makes his stand
In the auditorium
Looking on she sings the songs
The words she knows, the tune
she hums

ROD STEWART
"Maggie May"

"'Maggie May' was more or less a true story, about the first woman I had sex with, at the Beaulieu Jazz Festival," Rod Stewart said. It recounts an affair with an older woman, from the point of view of a young man who has to be back in school in late September. (Stewart was 16 when he had the affair.)

Stewart was still the lead singer of the Faces when "Maggie May" came out, and was recording his second album, Every Picture Tells a Story. He was close to finishing the album, but was still short a song. "['Maggie May'] nearly got left off because the label said it didn't have a melody," Stewart recalls. "I said, 'Well, we've run out of time now, these are all the tracks we've recorded.' They said, 'All right, then, bring it on.'" The song was originally released as a B-side to "Reason to Believe," but a deejay in Milwaukee, Wisconsin flipped it over; Stewart liked to say that if the deejay hadn't, Stewart would have had to go back to his original job, digging ditches for graves.

"Maggie May" ended up being a #1 hit in the both the U.S. and the U.K., as did the entire album; the achievement put Stewart in a small club that included the Beatles and Simon and Garfunkel. Soon, the Faces were being billed as "Rod Stewart and the Faces" and would disband. Years later, Stewart still seemed surprised about "Maggie's" success: "I still can't see how the single is such a big hit. It has no melody. Plenty of character and nice chords, but no melody."

1971

"Changes"

DAVID BOWIE

125 - David Bowie performing as Ziggy Stardust at the Hammersmith Odeon in London.

126/127 - David Bowie as Ziggy Stardust; the single "Starman" first put Ziggy on the pop map.

"The one thing I remember from that time," said David Bowie about his early concerts, "was how many couples went in for extremely heavy petting at our shows. Inhibitions seemed to fall off like leaves at the gig entrance door." No one had seen anything quite like David Bowie during the Ziggy Stardust tour in 1972, when he broke out the glam-rock costumes and stagecraft for the first time. There had been makeup and over-the-top performances in rock – see Alice Cooper – but no one had brought the seriousness of purpose that Bowie did, or the number of fantastic songs.

"Changes" was from Bowie's hippie-ish album Hunky Dory. The song "started out as a parody of a nightclub song, a kind of throwaway"; he worked it up for Hunky Dory with Rick Wakeman on keyboards and Mick Ronson behind the strings. The saxophone solo at the end was played by Bowie.

The song became Bowie's manifesto in later years. Lyrics such as "So I turned myself to face me / But I've never caught a glimpse" became about Bowie's mutable idea of identity. Young fans, meanwhile, deeply related to lines such as "And these children that you spit on / As they try to change their worlds / Are immune to your consultations / They're quite aware of what they're going through."

The song's importance to Bowie fans only grew with age; by 1975, it was a song they demanded. "'Changes' turned into this monster that nobody would stop asking for at concerts: 'Dye-vid, Dye-vid' do Changes!'" Bowie said. "I had no idea it would become such a popular thing. "

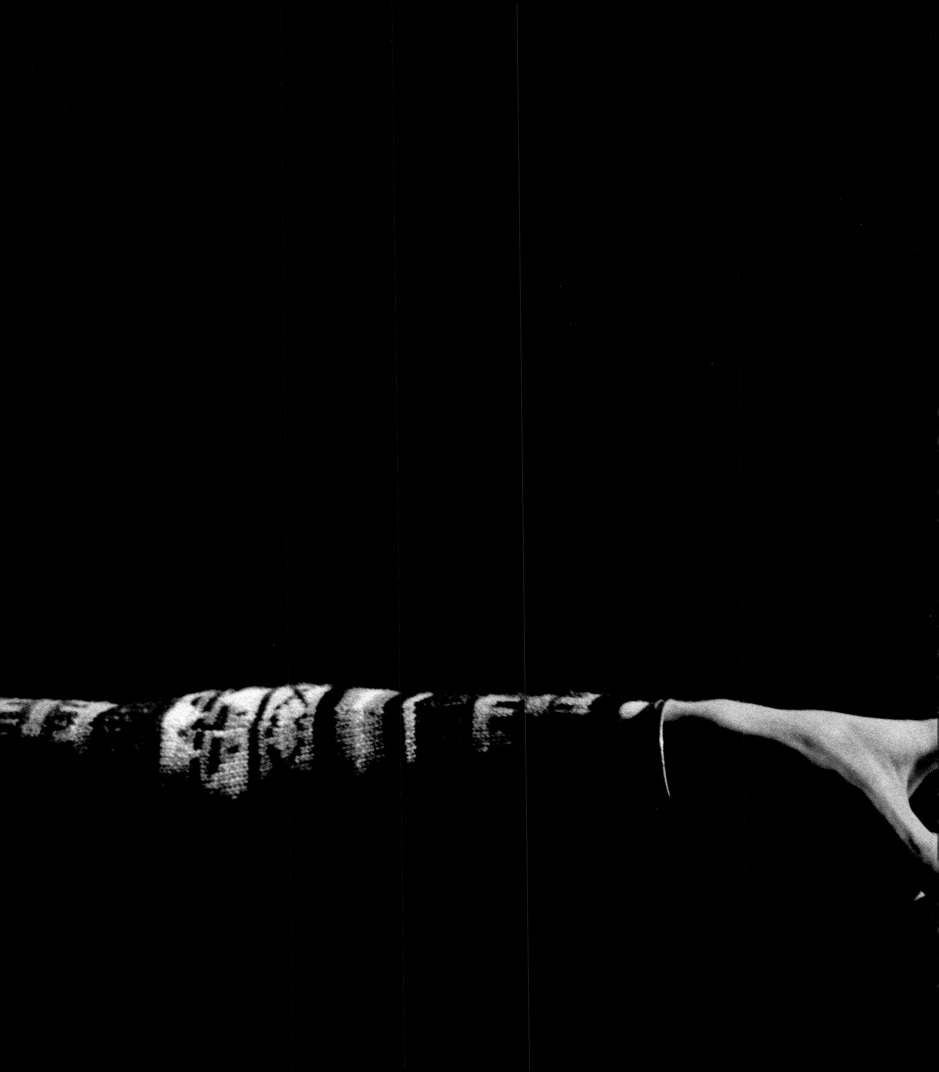

Heart Of Gold

"Heart of Gold"

NEIL YOUNG

129 - Neil Young performing in London; the album "Harvest" marked his commercial high point.

"I think Harvest is probably the finest record I've made," Neil Young said. The most commercially successful album of Young's career was, in a sense, a fluke. Young hurt his back badly in 1971, and had a difficult time even picking up an electric guitar. He was in Nashville to play Johnny Cash's variety show, so he decided to cut an album of mellow, acoustic songs using some of the city's crack session players. The centerpiece of Harvest was a gentle song about a man searching for virtue and kindness in a harsh world: "I've been to Hollywood / I've been to Redwood / I've crossed the ocean for a heart of gold."

James Taylor and Linda Ronstadt were also in town to appear on the Johnny Cash show, so Young asked them to join in the harmonies at the end of the song. (Young also handed Taylor a banjo to play; it was the first time Taylor had ever picked one up.) Some of the Nashville musicians didn't appreciate Young's simple, almost primitive arrangements: "He hires some of the best musicians in the world," said drummer Kenny Buttery, "and has them play as stupid as they possibly can." But Harvest has a warm pulse and front-to-back sweetness that audiences responded to by the millions. One person who didn't appreciate the song was Bob Dylan, one of Young's heroes, who thought that it sounded too much like him. "I used to hate it when it came on the radio," Dylan said. "I always liked Neil Young, but it bothered me every time I listened to 'Heart of Gold.'" And despite pressure from his record label to record another mega-hit, Young didn't dwell in the song's soft-rock territory for long. "This song put me in the middle of the road," Young said. "Traveling there soon became a bore so I headed for the ditch."

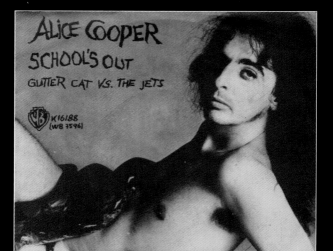

1972

ALICE COOPER
"School's Out"

"There were lots of good guys in rock," said Alice Cooper (born Vincent Furnier), "but there were no rock and roll villains." Cooper and his powerful band (lead guitarist Glen Buxton, rhythm guitarist Michael Bruce, bass player Dennis Dunaway and drummer Neal Smith) invented "shock rock," a mix of horror movies, vaudeville and heavy guitars that thrilled millions of fans in the early Seventies, and helped give birth to heavy metal's mix of fright and showmanship.

Cooper got the term "school's out" from an old Bowery Boys movie; it was street slang for "get with it." But there's no question what the song is about. "What's the greatest three minutes of your life?" Cooper asked. "There's two times during the year. One is Christmas morning, when you're just getting ready to open the presents. The next one is the last three minutes of the last day of school when you're sitting there and it's like a slow fuse burning. I said, 'If we can catch that three minutes in a song, it's going to be so big.'"

The children getting out of school in the summer of 1972 responded immediately to lines like "school's been blown to pieces"; adults enjoyed clever lyrics like "Well we got no class / And we got no principals." The capper was the children's chorus, which was producer Bob Ezrin's idea (he would reprise that idea in 1979, when he produced Pink Floyd's "Another Brick in the Wall"). Cooper knew he had hit his target: "When we did 'School's Out,' I knew we had just done the national anthem," he said later. "I've become the Francis Scott Key of the last day of school."

132/133 - Cooper at the Olympia Theater; Cooper wrote "School's Out" knowing it would become an anthem for students.

133 - Cooper on stage; he was known for using vaudevillian stage props such as guillotines and fake blood.

1972

DEEP PURPLE
Smoke on the water
Smoke on the water(live)

DEEP PURPLE
"Smoke on the Water"

Deep Purple guitarist Ritchie Blackmore wrote the central riff to "Smoke on the Water" during a jam session. He was almost embarrassed to bring it to the rest of the band because it was so simple, but his chugging, elemental hook ended up being a progression every beginning guitar player tries to puzzle out, one that has come to define Seventies hard rock.

The lyrics are a very specific recounting of a fire at the Montreux Jazz Festival that the band witnessed. They were in town to record their album Machine Head, and a fan

accidentally set the fire by shooting off a flare gun at a Frank Zappa gig. (The fire starter is memorialized in the song as "some stupid with a flare gun.") The "smoke" was the casino burning, and the "water" was Lake Geneva.

Among the real-life characters in the song are Claude Nobs, the founder of the Montreux Jazz Festival, who is referred to as "Funky Claude" who was "running in and out and pulling kids out the ground." "Deep Purple were watching the whole fire from their hotel window," Nobs recalled, "and they said, Oh

my God, look what happened. Poor Claude, and there's no casino anymore!' They were supposed to record the new album there. Finally I found a place in a little abandoned hotel next to my house and we made a temporary studio for them. One day they were coming up for dinner at my house and they said, 'Claude, we did a little surprise for you, but it's not going to be on the album. It's a tune called 'Smoke On the Water.' So I listened to it. I said, 'You're crazy. It's going to be a huge thing.' Now there's no guitar player in the world who doesn't know it."

With a few red lights and a few old beds
We make a place to sweat
No matter what we get out of this
I know, I know we'll never forget
Smoke on the water, a fire in the sky ,
smoke on the water

136 - Roger Glover and Ian Gillian onstage in Copenhagen, Denmark in 1972.

137 - Guitarist Ritchie Blackmore; Blackmore always thought the "Smoke on the Water" riff was too simple.

1973

KNOCKIN' ON HEAVEN'S DOOR

139 - Bob Dylan's albums became more idiosyncratic after his motorcycle accident in the late Sixties.

BOB DYLAN
"Knockin' on Heaven's Door"

Bob Dylan hadn't released an album in three years when he went to Mexico with Kris Kristofferson for a bit role in director Sam Peckinpah's film Pat Garrett and Billy the Kid. Dylan seemed ill at ease on the set, harassed by overzealous fans, but toward the end of the experience he said, "I want now to make movies. I've never been this close to movies before. I'll make a hell of a movie after this."

Dylan never did make a great movie, but he did record a wonderful soundtrack to Pat Garrett, recording in Mexico City and in the States. Playing with local Mexican musicians, Dylan recorded achingly pretty soundtrack songs such as "Billy"; he found the comfort level he had been missing in the studio, and set the stage for future masterpieces such as Planet Waves and Blood on the Tracks.

The towering achievement on the Pat Garrett soundtrack was "Knockin' on Heaven's Door," the story of a dying lawman who sings, "Mama, take this badge off of me / I can't use it anymore. / It's gettin' dark, too dark to see / I feel like I'm knockin' on heaven's door." Few people have seen Peckinpah's film but "Knockin'" has been covered by legions of bands: the most famous version is by Guns N' Roses, Eric Clapton recorded a reggae-flavored version, and everyone from U2 to Dolly Parton has played it in concert.

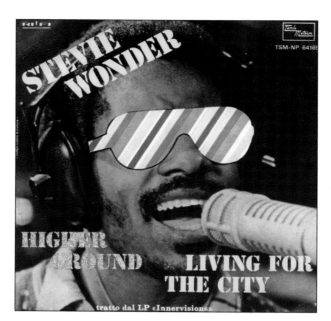

TSM·NP 64169

STEVIE WONDER

HIGHER GROUND ... LIVING FOR THE CITY

tratto dal LP «Innervisions»

STEVIE WONDER
"Living for the City"

With the album Innervisions, Stevie Wonder addressed race and poverty in America head-on for the first time in his career – and because he was Stevie Wonder, he did it better than anybody else. "Living for the City" is a song that spans both hope and immeasurable sadness; it follows a young man who grows up in "hard times Mississippi" and moves to New York City, only to fall prey to hustlers and end up in jail.

Wonder played all the instruments, and sampled actual street sounds for the spoken word section in the middle of the song. The police officer who jails the protagonists (saying, "Get in that cell, nigger") was a janitor at the recording studio whom Wonder pressed into service.

"Innervisions gives my own perspective of what's happening in my world," Wonder said, adding, "That's why it took me seven months to get together – I did all the lyrics – and that's why I think it's my most personal album. I don't care if it sells only five copies – this is the way I feel." To give journalists a feel for what he was experiencing, members of the press were blindfolded and driven to a special album release party, where they listened to songs from the album and handled musical instruments without the benefit of eyesight. Wonder would win three Grammys for Innervisions.

143 - ZZ Top formed in 1969 in Houston, Texas; they reinvented themselves in the 1980s with hits like "Legs."

ZZ TOP
"La Grange"

As the saying goes, rock and roll is based on "three chords, a guitar and the truth." But in the case of "La Grange," ZZ Top (guitarist Billy Gibbons, bassist Dusty Hill and drummer Frank Beard) needed only one chord. The entire song – which is based on John Lee Hooker's "Boogie Chillen" – is a variation on one blistering blues chord. It was ZZ Top's biggest hit up to that point. It became a big radio hit and reached #41 on the Billboard singles chart.

The song tells the story of a whorehouse called the Chicken Ranch on the outskirts of the Texas town of La Grange. "Did you ever see the movie, 'The Best Little Whorehouse in Texas'?" Hill asked. "That's what it's about. I went there when I was 13. A lot of boys in Texas, when it's time to be a guy, went there and had it done. Fathers took their sons there. You couldn't cuss in there. You couldn't drink. It had an air of respectability. Oil field workers

and senators would both be there."

Unfortunately, the song "La Grange" was so successful that it got the brothel shut down. As Hill remembers, a reporter from Houston "stirred up so much shit that it had to close. We wrote this song and put it out, and it was out maybe three months before they closed it. It pissed me off. It was a whorehouse, but anything that lasts a hundred years, there's got to be a reason."

Rumour spreadin' a-'round in that Texas town/'bout that shack outside La Grange/and you know what I'm talkin' about./Just let me know if you wanna go/to that home out on the range./They gotta lotta nice girls ah.

1973

BOB MARLEY AND THE WAILERS

"Get Up, Stand Up" is recognized as one of the greatest political songs of all time, but for the Wailers, it was a defense of Rastafarianism – an attack on the belief that you should spend your life trying to get into heaven by praying to a monotheistic deity. Whatever the ideology behind it, "Stand Up" is pure inspiration; it's become a theme song on the level of Pete Seeger's "We Shall Overcome" for protests all over the world.

The Wailers (Bob Marley, Peter Tosh and Bunny Livingston)

recorded "Stand Up" for the Burnin' album – the last album the original three Wailers would collaborate on – at Harry J. Studios in Kingston, Jamaica. (By chance, the Rolling Stones were working next door on their album Goat's Head Soup; at one point, Mick Jagger interrupted the Wailers' recording session to ask if Chris Blackwell could help get his friend Anita Pallenberg, who had been busted for drugs in Ocho Rios, out of trouble.)

Marley and Tosh co-wrote the song; Marley was a fan of the

socially conscious soul-pop group War, and tried to approximate the funky shuffle of the song "Slipping into Darkness" on "Get Up, Stand Up." Marley sang most of it, but the fiery Tosh sang the climactic verse, and took the song to the breaking point. A few years later, in 1977, Tosh would record a solo version of the song that would become even better known than the original.

"Get Up, Stand Up" would be the last song Marley would ever perform in concert, in September 1980.

1973

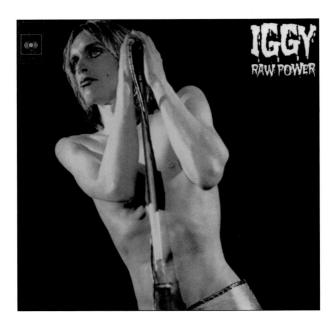

THE STOOGES
"Search and Destroy"

"I'm a street-walkin' cheetah with a heart full of napalm." With this lyric, the Stooges took their assault on old-school hippie rock to a new level of intensity. "Search and Destroy" was the lead-off track on their proto-punk masterpiece Raw Power, and perhaps the most ferocious moment from a band that specialized in them.

Iggy Pop says he took the concept of "search and destroy" from a Time magazine article about the Vietnam War. "I used to read Time obsessively, because they were the representatives of the ultimate establishment to me," said Pop, "so I liked to look in there and see what they were talking about, and then I'd use that inventory in other ways. That's what I was doing in that song." Pop's lyrics are a mission statement for nihilistic youth: "I'm the runaway son of a nuclear A-bomb / I am the world's forgotten boy / The one who searches and destroys."

"The thing about 'forgotten boy' was basically a way to express my disgust," Iggy said. Years later, he said one of the targets for his anger was the music business: "Music as a branch of the entertainment industry was becoming an old cheese. It was about a bunch of people at the top manipulating certain institutional positions with the smug confidence that 'kids' at the bottom would swallow whatever they put out. They thought they could sell shit if there was money in it but they'd forgotten about the simple truth that any kid can see."

148 - Iggy Pop was famous for his onstage antics – most notoriously, cutting himself with glass.

148/149 - Scott Asheton, Iggy Pop and James Williamson of the Stooges live in San Francisco.

1975

BRUCE SPRINGSTEEN
"Born to Run"

"Bruce Springsteen's work epitomizes rock's deepest values: desire, the need for freedom and the search to find yourself," said his longtime friend Jackson Browne. He added, "[In] his songs there is a generosity and a willingness to portray even the simplest aspects of our lives in a dramatic and committed way." "Born to Run" is the ultimate example of Springsteen's fire and commitment: four and a half minutes of Phil Spector-sized thunder and dreams of rock and roll escape.

"I had enormous ambitions for it," Springsteen said. "I wanted to make the greatest rock record I'd ever heard." This one song took three and a half months to cut; there were a dozen guitar overdubs, and Springsteen was spending his record label's money at a dangerous pace (it's said that engineer Jimmy Iovine had to hide the studio bills from Columbia Records executives.) Springsteen has said that the lyrics are based on getting out of Asbury Park, New Jersey ("The amusement park rises bold and stark / Kids are huddled on the beach in a mist" refers to the town's points of

interest). But "Born to Run" appeals to anybody with a sense of longing and dreams and visions to protect. "I don't know how important the settings are," Springsteen said. "It's the idea behind the settings. It could be New Jersey, it could California, it could be Alaska."

"Born to Run" spent 11 weeks on the Billboard Singles chart and peaked at #23; to this day Springsteen almost never plays a show without performing it. "Bruce has always worked on a large scale," Browne said. "A scale that is nothing short of heroic."

152 - Bruce Springsteen and the E Street Band live at Alex Cooley's Electric Ballroom in Atlanta, Georgia.

153 - Springsteen: Critic Jon Landau famously wrote, "I have seen rock and roll's future, and it is Bruce Springsteen."

155 - Bruce Springsteen and the E Street Band live at Monmouth College in Long Branch, New Jersey.

Wendy let me in I wanna be your friend
I want to guard your dreams and visions
Just wrap your legs 'round these velvet rims
and strap your hands 'cross my engines
Together we could break this trap
We'll run till we drop, baby we'll never go back

AEROSMITH
"Sweet Emotion"

Aerosmith bassist Tom Hamilton was driving to the studio with the band's producer, Jack Douglas. "I've got something," Hamilton told him. "You've gotta hear it." That "something" was the rolling bass line to "Sweet Emotion" – one of the most dramatic openings in Seventies rock.

The riff almost didn't make it onto the album, though. The band was in the last day of recording their classic album Toys when Douglas asked, "Does anybody have any spare riffs lying around?" Hamilton volunteered, and Douglas liked it. So Hamilton said he "smoked a bowl or two and wrote the arrangements."

"Sweet Emotion" turned out to be the band's most ferocious rocker. The key to the song is in the tension between the off-kilter bass line and ominous, almost psychedelic sounds in the background, and the barn-burning verses and chorus. "That sucking sound on 'Sweet Emotion' is a combination of hi-hat cymbal, backward clapping and 'masking' the words "Thanks, Frank," Douglas explained. "Frank" was Frank Connelly, the band's unpopular manager. Douglas continued, "We used to take a guitar riff, play it backward and learn it, a Beatles technique that John Lennon taught me. Being an engineer, I got to steal from the best guys."

The harsh sentiments in Steven Tyler's verses – "You talk about things that nobody cares / You're wearing out things that nobody wears / You call my name but I gotta make clear / I can't say baby where I'll be in a year" – were all directed at Joe Perry's first wife, Elyssa. Her crime? "She was doing all his drugs," Tyler said. "Before she came along, I was doing his drugs. It was a big problem." "Sweet Emotion" became Aerosmith's biggest hit yet, spending eight weeks on the charts. It remains a staple of classic rock radio.

Sweet Emotion
Sweet Emotion

You talk about things that nobody cares
You're wearing out things that nobody wears
You're calling my name but I gotta make clear
I can't say baby where I'll be in a year

158 - Steven Tyler and guitarist Joe Perry of Aerosmith at the Hammersmith Odeon in London.

159 - Steven Tyler, Tom Hamilton, Brad Whitford and Joe Perry; "Sweet Emotion" was almost an afterthought for the band.

1975

QUEEN "Bohemian Rhapsody"

It is one of the most ambitious songs in rock – a fantastical trip through piano balladry, opera, guitar crescendos and hard rock. Queen guitarist Brian May says it was the brainchild of singer Freddie Mercury. "It was all in Freddie's mind," he said. Mercury wrote the bulk of "Bohemian Rhapsody" in his West London home. Producer Roy Thomas Baker recalls hearing it for the first time: "[Mercury] played the beginning on the piano, then stopped and said, 'And this is where the opera section comes in!'"

In its day, it was the most expensive single ever recorded. The band recorded it in three weeks, using no less than six recording studios. Queen pushed the limits of recording technology at the time, piling on layer after layer of audio; May recalls that the recording tape was thin and almost transparent after they had crammed all the tracks on it.

"I remember Freddie coming in with loads of bits of paper and pounding on the piano," May said. "He'd worked out the harmonies in his head." The band would record ten to twelve hours of vocal parts a day for the intricate opera section, with May taking the low parts, Mercury taking the middle, and band member Roger Taylor taking the high parts. Taylor says they wanted to make "a wall of sound that starts down and goes all the way up."

"Bohemian Rhapsody" was a huge hit when it was released; the single sold more than a million copies in its first year – eventually becoming the third-best-selling single of all time in the U.K. – and remained at the #1 spot on the U.K. singles chart for nine weeks.

162/163 - Freddie Mercury and Brian May: "Bohemian Rhapsody" combined opera, hard rock and balladry.

"Blitzkrieg Bop"

THE RAMONES

165 - Johnny and Joey Ramone live on Don Kirshner's rock variety show in Los Angeles, California.

"Every rock and roll generation needs reminding of why it picks up a guitar in the first place," wrote Lenny Kaye about the Ramones, "and four non-brothers from the borough of Queens had a concept that was almost too perfect." That concept? Bowl haircuts, leather jackets, ripped blue jeans, and a battery of three-chord songs that stopped for no man.

"Blitzkrieg Bop," the first single on their first album, was a salute to the Ramones' fans and the energy of rock and roll. It was written mostly by Tommy Ramone; he came up with the famous chant "Hey! Ho! Let's go!" after hearing the Bay City Rollers' "Saturday Night" (which has the chorus "S-A-T-U-R-D-A-Y night!") and deciding it would be cool to have a chant. Bassist Dee Dee Ramone came up with the line "Shoot 'em in the back now." The lyric was originally "They're shouting in the back now," but Dee Dee liked his idea better.

The key throughout was simplicity. "Our music is an answer to the early Seventies when artsy people with big egos would do vocal harmonies and play long guitar solos and get called geniuses," said Tommy Ramone when the band was first breaking. "That was bullshit. We play rock and roll. We don't do solos."

"Blitzkrieg Bop" never made it on the charts, but it was the tip of the spear of a new movement, punk rock. The Ramones played the U.K. in 1976 and 1977, and it almost seemed as if every audience member started a band: half of the future U.K. punk bands of the Seventies, including the Sex Pistols and the Clash, were in the crowd. "If anything, the Ramones affirmed that if they could do it, you could do it," wrote Kaye. "Just be resolute. Count to four."

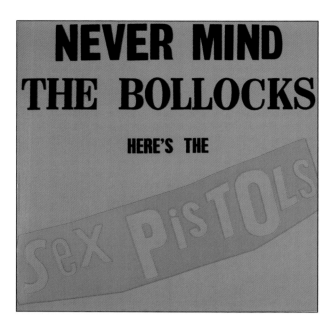

1977

NEVER MIND THE BOLLOCKS

HERE'S THE

Sex Pistols

167 - The Sex Pistols became notorious in the U.K. after a profane confrontation with a TV talk show host.

168/169 - The Sex Pistols onstage in Huddersfield, England; at one early club show, future members of the Clash, the Buzzcocks and Joy Division were in the audience.

SEX PISTOLS

"Anarchy in the U.K."

"Anarchy in the U.K." was "the clarion call of a generation," said Colin Newman of the band Wire. It was a burst of rebellion and guitars that announced the arrival of punk; on a certain level, it's the perfect rock song: loud, brash, self-destructive – and world-changing. "I am an Antichrist / And I am an anarchist," sang Johnny Rotten, "Don't know what I want but I know how to get it / I wanna destroy / the passerby / Cause I wanna be anarchy."

The Sex Pistols were an assortment of local musicians assembled by impresario Malcolm McLaren and led by a provocative street kid named John Lydon. As the story goes, guitarist Steve Jones dubbed him Johnny Rotten because of his bad teeth. "Anarchy" was the Sex Pistols' first single. Like most of their songs, Lydon said, it was the outgrowth of pure working class frustration: "['Anarchy'] flowed quite naturally to me," he said. "You can't ever underestimate the sheer driving energy poverty will bring you. Government, schools, the lot, tell you that you don't count. You are scum. Go with flow or else. That's an incredible driving energy, to be better than their estimation of you."

The band had played "Anarchy" live for almost a year and, having just been signed to major label EMI Records, were taking their first uneasy crack at recording. "We spent a long time recording that with [manager] Malcolm McLaren just saying how it's got to be faster," said Jones. "It's a myth that these guys couldn't play their instruments," Billie Joe Armstrong of Green Day told Rolling Stone, adding, "Steve Jones is one of the best guitarists of all time, as far as I'm concerned."

The circumstances around "Anarchy"'s release gave it even more notoriety. In November 1977, the Sex Pistols went on a popular British talk show with punk friends including Siouxsie Siouix (soon to be of Siouxie and the Banshees). The bandmates were drinking before the show and got into an argument with Grundy, and Jones ended up spitting obscenities at him. After a British tabloid firestorm of controversy, the Sex Pistols were dropped by EMI. Soon they were being denounced in Parliament, and their legend was secure.

"I don't understand it," Rotten said. "All we're trying to do is destroy something."

I am an anti-christ
I am an anarchist
Don't know what I want but I know how to get it
I wanna destroy the passer by, 'cause I
I wanna be anarchy!

1977

QUEEN
"We Will Rock You"

As the story goes, Sid Vicious of the Sex Pistols walked into the wrong recording studio one day, and bumped into Freddie Mercury of Queen sitting at the piano. "Still bringing ballet to the masses, are you?" he asked Mercury sarcastically. "Oh yes, Mr. Ferocious, dear," replied Mercury. "We are doing our best."

But soon Queen would shake the rafters of rock radio with "We Will Rock You," one of the most elemental songs they – or anybody – would ever record. It

consists almost entirely of loud echoing foot stomps, torrid guitar and a mammoth sing-along chant.

Brian May wrote the song, after deciding he wanted to "create a song that the audience could participate in." They had recently played a show in Stafford, England: "We did an encore and then went off," May said, "and instead of just keeping clapping, they sang "You'll Never Walk Alone" to us, and we were just completely knocked out and taken aback – it was quite an

emotional experience really, and I think these chant things are in some way connected with that."

The band recorded "We Will Rock You" in an old church in North London. "We were very lucky," May said. "It already had a nice sound. And there were some old boards lying around, but they just seemed ideal to stamp on." May used his degree in astrophysics in creating the song's massive thumping sound. "Being a physicist, I said, 'Suppose there were a thousand people doing this; what would be

happening?' And I thought, well, you would be hearing them stamping. You would also be hearing a little bit of an effect, which is due to the distance that they are from you. So I put lots of individual repeats on them. Not an echo but a single repeat at various distances."

"Much later on, people designed a machine to do this," said May, "but that's what we did." To this day, "Rock You" is still played at large sporting events, and crowds of thousands still stomp along.

172 - Freddie Mercury at the Oakland Coliseum in 1977; "Bohemian Rhapsody" combined opera, hard rock and balladry.

173 - Brian May was Queen's other mastermind; he's still considered to be one of rock's greatest guitarists.

Buddy you're a boy make
a big noise
Playin' in the street gonna be
a big man some day
You got mud on yo' face
You big disgrace
Kickin' your can all over
the place

We will we will rock you
We will we will rock you

174/175 - Roger Taylor, John Deacon, Freddie Mercury and Brian
May (left to right) of Queen at a TV taping.

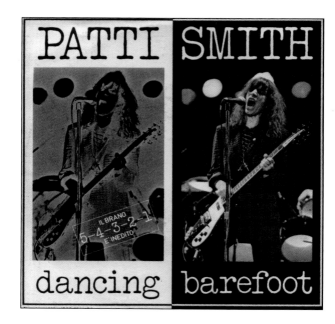

PATTI SMITH GROUP
"Dancing Barefoot"

"She is benediction / She is addicted to thee / She is the root connection / She is connecting with he." No other song in rock approaches love and sex with the same mystical, uplifting fervor as "Dancing Barefoot." "I think sex is one of the five highest sensations one can experience," Smith said in 1978. "A very high orgasm is a way of communion with our creator."

Patti Smith had already upended most people's idea of a woman rocker before "Barefoot," with albums such as Horses and Easter. Now, in a happy relationship with Fred "Sonic" Smith, the former guitarist of the MC5, she put the same poetry and commitment into

documenting their relationship. ("Barefoot" and "Frederick" – another song from her 1979 album Wave – were dedicated to Smith; "Barefoot" was also dedicated, on the Wave album sleeve, to "the rites of the heroine; and to Jeanne Hébuterne, mistress to Amedeo Modigliani.")

After a fallow period during the Eighties, when Patti took time off to be a wife and mother, her influence became more obvious to a generation of Nineties post-punk rockers – especially women in rock bands. "Patti Smith saved my life," said Courtney Love. Shirley Manson of Garbage said: "I was about 19 when I first heard a Patti Smith

record. I remember sitting there, very taken by the sound of her voice's ferocious delivery. She was the complete opposite of the images that were pumped into me as a child, of what I was supposed to aspire to in a woman."

After the death of Fred "Sonic" Smith in 1994, Patti reentered musical life, recording four new studio albums and touring; she was inducted into the Rock and Roll Hall of Fame in 2007. "Dancing Barefoot" has been affirmed as one of her greatest songs, covered by bands such as U2 and Pearl Jam. "I found it very wonderful to hear different interpretations," Smith said. "It helped keep the music alive."

1979

181 - Frank Zappa in France; Zappa's influences included avant-garde composers and 1950s rhythm and blues.

182/183 - Zappa brought a new level of orchestration and technical virtuosity to 1960s and 1970s rock.

FRANK ZAPPA
"Catholic Girls"

No musician pushed rock further into the territory of pure jazz and classical orchestration than Frank Zappa – or took rock guitar into more new, formerly alien places. "I think he was the best electric guitar player, other than Jimi Hendrix," said Trey Anastasio of Phish. "Zappa conceptualized the instrument in a completely different way, rhythmically and sonically. Every boundary that was possible on the guitar was examined by him."

"Catholic Girls" – part of Zappa's rock opera Joe's Garage – was the quintessential mix of his influences: a goofball trip into the world of randy schoolgirls and the musicians they love, informed by freak rock, Fifties music and avant garde composers such as Edgar Varese. The chorus was catchy but also precise and harmonically interesting; the lyrics were bawdy ("Do you know how they go ... after the show?").

The most important thing about "Catholic Girls" – and all of Zappa's music –was the possibilities it unlocked in the minds of musicians. "Zappa gave me the faith that anything in music was possible," Anastasio said. "He demystified the whole thing for musicians in my generation: 'Look, these are just instruments. Find out what the range is, and start writing.'"

With a tiny little mustache
Catholic girls
Do you know how they go?
Catholic girls
In the rectory basement
Father rileys a fairy
But it don't bother mary
Catholic girls
At the cyo
Catholic girls
Do you know how they go?
Catholic girls
There can be no replacement
How do they go, after the show?

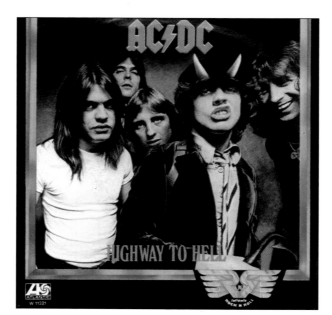

AC/DC
"Highway to Hell"

"I'll go on record as saying [AC/DC] are the greatest rock and roll band of all time," said producer Rick Rubin. "They didn't write emotional lyrics. They didn't play emotional songs. The emotion is all in that groove. And that groove is timeless."

"Highway to Hell" is one of the band's crushing high points. It's one of the ultimate rock and roll road songs – and a mission statement for the hard rock lifestyle: "Living easy, living free / Season ticket on a one-way ride / Asking nothing, leave me be."

The song was written by the late singer Bon Scott, probably after driving on a treacherous stretch of road from his hometown of Fremantle, Australia to a bar called The Raffles. There were so many accidents along one hilly section of the road that it was called the highway to hell. Lyrics such as "Ain't nothing I would rather do / Going down, party time / My friends are gonna be there too" were probably about Scott going to drink with his friends at The Raffles. Guitarist Angus Young said it was about the grind of being on tour all the time: "a fucking highway to hell." Scott said in 1978: "I've been on the road for 13 years. Planes,

hotels, groupies, booze ... they all scrape something from you."

Scott drank himself to death in 1980, shortly after finishing the album that shares the song's name. "Highway to Hell" was the first AC/DC song to reach the U.S. charts; the album Highway to Hell has sold more than seven million copies. "Highway to Hell is probably the most natural sounding rock record I've ever heard," Rubin said. "There's so little adornment. For me, it's the embodiment of rock and roll. It sounds simple, but what AC/DC did is almost impossible to duplicate."

Living easy/Loving free/Season ticket for a one way ride/Asking nothing/Leave me be/Taken everything in my stride/Don't need reason/Don't need rhyme/Ain't nothin' I would rather do/Going down/By the time/My friends are gonna be there too, eh/I'm on a highway to hell/On the highway to hell

1979

"Sultans of Swing"

DIRE STRAITS

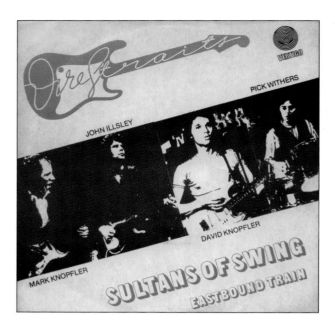

189 - Dire Straits (left to right): John Illsley, Terry Williams, Mark Knopfler, Hal Lindes and Alan Clark.

Dire Straits were an anomaly when they released "Sultans of Swing." When they first hit the scene, one Rolling Stone reviewer wrote: "It's almost as if they were aware that their forte has nothing to do with what's currently happening in the industry, but couldn't care less." "Sultans," the band's first single, was the epitome of that outlook: its gentle up-tempo groove was too smart for soft rock, too electric to be folk, and utterly disconnected with the rock world in 1979, which consisted of album rock, punk, New Wave and disco.

The revelation was leadman Mark Knopfler's liquid, twangy guitar playing, which took on a Spanish lilt during his solo; the song almost immediately made Knopfler a guitar hero. Knopfler reportedly got the idea for "Sultans" after ducking into a bar on a rainy night and watching a mediocre band perform in front of a handful of drinkers. At the end of the set, the lead singer announced, "Good night and thank you. We are the sultans of swing." The band recorded a five-song demo tape which included "Sultans"; it was already getting radio play and causing a minor sensation in London when they were signed to EMI.

Still, many people didn't see how a band that seemed so far from the norm could succeed in the long term. The same reviewer called their first album "one of those quietly subversive albums whose sober lucidity reeks of rapid obscurity. It doesn't deserve such a sad fate." Luckily, fate was kind.

You get a shiver in the dark/It's raining in the park but meantime/South of the river you stop and you hold everything/A band is blowing Dixie double four time

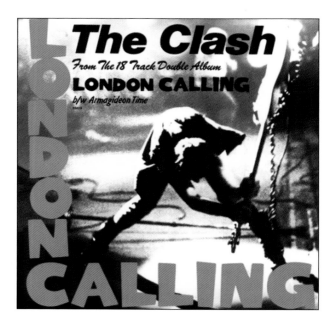

THE CLASH
"London Calling"

"The ice age is coming / The sun's zooming in / Meltdown expected / The wheat is growing thin / A nuclear error / But I have no fear / 'Cause London is drowning / And I, I live by the river": With "London Calling," the Clash singlehandedly took punk rock beyond its heretofore mostly personal, emotional concerns, engaging current events like the accident at Three Mile Island nuclear power plant (the "nuclear error") with rock and roll fury. The band was also taking their sound to a new place, reaching beyond punk's standard I-IV-V chord progressions.

In 1979, "We felt that we were struggling, about to slip down a slope or something, grasping with our fingernails," said Joe Strummer, "and there was no one to help us." The band had no manager and was in debt. Meanwhile, the U.K. was facing widespread joblessness and little sign of relief.

"London Calling" – the title of the song comes from the BBC World Service radio identification – was the band venting its desperation, and putting it in a broader context. The line "phony Beatlemania has bitten the dust" is Strummer referring to the Broadway musical show "Beatlemania," a simulation of Beatles songs. Strummer was bemoaning the shallow side of Seventies culture. The chorus "London is drowning / And I live by the river" refers to a local concern: "They say that if the Thames ever flooded, we'd all be underwater," Mick Jones said. (Jones did point out that Strummer was living in a tall apartment building at the time, "so he wouldn't have drowned.") The single reached #11 in the U.K. (it never charted in the United States) and was the first Clash song to reach the charts internationally.

The ice age is coming,
the sun's zooming in
Meltdown expected,
the wheat is growing thin
Engines stop running,
but I have no fear
Cause London is drowning
I live by the river

195 - Blondie (left to right):
Clem Burke, Chris Stein, Debbie
Harry, Nigel Harrison, Frank
Infante and Jimmy Destri.

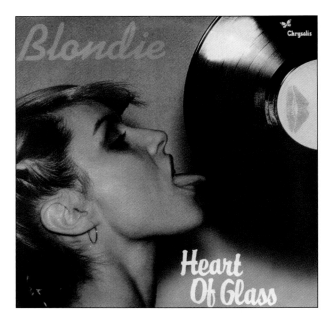

1979

BLONDIE "Heart of Glass"

"Heart of Glass" is a perfect blend of New Wave and disco – a sign that there was hope for sexy, smart pop after the turmoil of Seventies punk. When it came out, some punk diehards call Blondie sellouts for making a disco song, but the songwriting team (and romantic pair) of Debbie Harry and Chris Stein had written the song years before. "We'd had 'Heart of Glass' kicking around for a while," Harry told Blender magazine in 2007. Says member Jimmy Destri: "We used to do 'Heart of Glass' to upset people."

"Everyone in the States was like, 'Blondie's gone disco,'" drummer Clem Burke recalled. He explained, "We all used to hang out at Club 82 in New York, which was essentially a gay disco. And in the early days, we used to play songs like 'Lady Marmalade' and 'I Feel Love.'"

Blondie had cut their teeth playing New York clubs such as CBGB's, and released two albums when they were signed to major label Chrysalis and put together with New Wave/pop producer Mike Chapman; he told them straightaway that he would make them a hit record. "Mike is a real hot chili pepper and very energetic and enthusiastic. Mike would strive for the technically impeccable take so we would do take after take," Harry said.

The band mulled different versions of "Heart of Glass," recording a reggae-style track before coming back to the dance idea. "Debbie said, 'Well, maybe it could be like a Donna Summer thing'," said Burke. The rest of the band wasn't sure, but Harry, Stein and Chapman insisted. Even so, they buried "Heart of Glass" on the second side of the album, not expecting it to be a hit. It was: "Glass" sold 1.5 million copies in a year, and New Wave had its first superstars.

Once I had a love and it was a gas, soon turned out Had a heart of glass/Seemed like the real thing, only to find /Mucho mistrust/Love's gone behind Once I had a love and it was divine/Soon found out I was losing my mind/It seemed like the real thing but I was so blind/Mucho mistrust/Love's gone behind

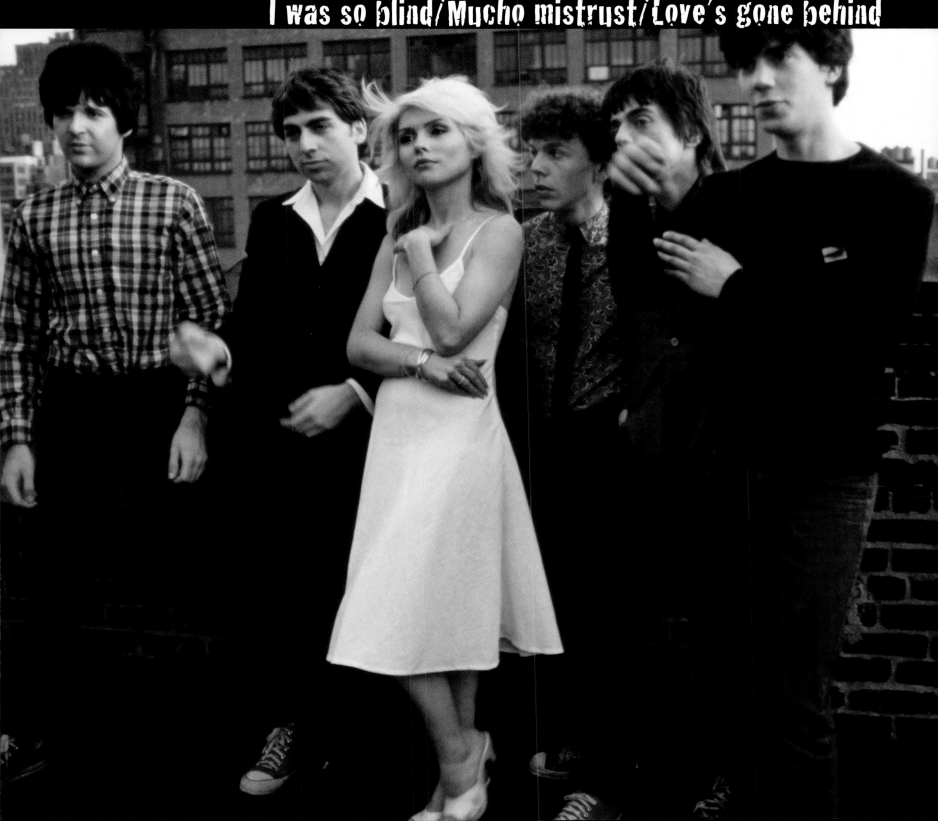

PINK FLOYD
"Comfortably Numb"

"Comfortably Numb" is the most emotional, uplifting song on Pink Floyd's classic album "The Wall" – but the lyrics are about drifting into a catatonic state. The soaring music came from guitarist David Gilmour; the dark verses came from bassist/bandleader Roger Waters.

Waters says lyrics such as "I hear you're feeling down / Well I can ease your pain / Get you on your feet again" come from an incident before a show in Philadelphia in 1977. He was suffering from undiagnosed hepatitis and was given a huge dose of tranquilizers. "I had stomach cramps so bad that I thought I wasn't able to go on," Waters told Mojo magazine. "A doctor backstage gave me a shot of something that I swear to God would have killed a fucking elephant. I did the whole show hardly able to raise my hand above my knee. He said it was a muscular relaxant. But it rendered me almost insensible."

The lines, "When I was a child I had a fever / My hands felt just like two balloons," were also based on Waters' life. "I remember having the flu or something, an infection with a temperature of 105° [40.6°C] and being delirious," he said. "It wasn't like the hands looked like balloons, but they looked way too big, frightening."

Gilmour's triumphant guitar solo was constructed in his usual way: he played five or six solos in the studio, then stitched together the best phrases for the final version. "I make a chart, putting ticks and crosses on different bars as I count through – two ticks if it's really good, one tick if it's good and cross if it's no go," Gilmour explained. "Then I just follow the chart, whipping one fader up, then another fader, jumping from phrase to phrase and trying to make a really nice solo all the way through."

"Comfortably Numb" was among the last songs Waters and Gilmour wrote together; Pink Floyd's next album, The Final Cut, was entirely Waters' vision. He would quit the band in 1986.

Hello? Is there anybody in there? Just nod if you can hear me.
Is there anyone at home? Come on, now, I hear you're feeling down.
Well I can ease your pain/Get you on your feet again. Relax.
I'll need some information first. Just the basic facts...

There is no pain
you are receding
A distant ship, smoke
on the horizon.
You are only coming
through in waves.
Your lips move but I can't hear
what you're saying.
When I was a child I had a fever
My hands felt just like
two balloons.
Now I've got that feeling
once again
I can't explain you
would not understand
This is not how I am.
I have become comfortably numb.

- After "The Wall," Pink Floyd became more fractured; "The Final Cut" was practically a Roger Waters solo album.

1981

R.E.M.
"Radio Free Europe"

If some of the lyrics to R.E.M.'s first single seem indecipherable, it's no accident: singer Michael Stipe says he mumbled them into the microphone because he "hadn't written any of the words yet" and some of the lines were "complete babbling." Lyrics or no, "Radio Free Europe" set the mold for the indie rock of the coming decades: smart but seemingly indifferent to professional recording techniques, full of atmosphere and strum. For a rock world that had been bloated by Seventies album rock, then disrupted by punk, this was a path forward.

"Europe" was recorded twice: first in 1981 for the indie label Hib-Tone. "We hated it," said guitarist Peter Buck. "It was mastered by a deaf man, apparently." He also called it "muddy and high-end." The band redid the song for their first album, Murmur, creating a cleaner version with drums "like Motown," according to Buck.

Now the band embraces both versions; even Buck admits "there's something to be said for the original sort of murky feeling" in the first version. "Europe" has been added to the American Library of Congress's National Recording Registry for setting "the pattern for later indie rock releases by breaking through on college radio in the face of mainstream radio's general indifference."

Raving station, beside yourself.
Keep me out of country in the word.
Deal the porch is leading us absurd.
Push that, push that, push that to the hull.
That this isn't nothing at all.

THE POLICE

EVERY BREATH YOU TAKE

THE POLICE
"Every Breath You Take"

It was a jarringly simple song for the Police – who were coming off of the maximalist thrills of songs like "Every Little Thing She Does is Magic" – and irresistibly catchy. The chord progression is tried and true, famously used in Ben E. King's "Stand by Me." "'Every Breath You Take' is an archetypal song," said Sting. "If you have a major chord followed by a relative minor, you're not original."

"It's ostensibly a love song, a very seductive romantic love song," he told Rolling Stone in 1988, "But it's about controlling somebody to the nth degree and monitoring their movements. It's not like 'Stand by Me,' which is this wonderful noble song that means just one thing. 'Every Breath You Take' is very ambiguous and quite wicked."

Sting wrote the song in Jamaica after separating from his first wife, Frances Tomelty. When it came time to record it, for the album Synchronicity, the band consciously stripped it down, taking off a big synthesizer part that drowned out the bass line, and replacing it with a mesmerizing Andy Summer guitar lick. Before the Eighties were over, Sting received a certification that "Every Breath You Take" had been played on the radio more than a million times. "It was as if one radio station had played it for five years nonstop. It was a staggering thought that this fucking evil song had permeated the airwaves." He later wrote "If You Love Somebody Set Them Free" for his first solo album, as an answer song.

Every breath you take/Every move you make/Every bond you break/
Every step you take/I'll be watching you/Every single day/
Every word you say/Every game you play/Every night you stay/
I'll be watching you

204 - Sting in London, 1983; the band would split after their Synchronicity album.

205 - The Police at their prime (left to right): Sting, Stewart Copeland and Andy Summers.

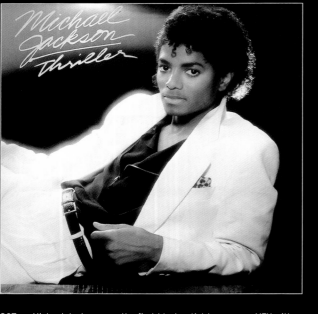

207 - Michael Jackson was the first black artist to conquer MTV with his "Beat It" video.

208-209 - The Jacksons onstage during the Victory Tour; Michael did it as a favor to his family.

"BILLIE JEAN"

MICHAEL JACKSON

"Billie Jean" is the most important record [Michael Jackson] made," said record label executive Antonio "L.A." Reid, "not only because of its commercial success but because of the musical depth of the record. It has more hooks in it than anything I've ever heard. Everything in that song was catchy, and every instrument was playing a different hook. You could separate it into twelve different musical pieces and I think you'd have twelve different hits."

Thriller producer Quincy Jones claimed that he pushed Jackson to write "Billie Jean": "We had everything in the can," Jones said, "and we were about to leave the studio. I played the tapes a few more times, and I didn't get that feeling. I told Michael that he had to write some stronger material. Everyone thought I was crazy. Over the next few days, he wrote 'Beat It' and 'Billie Jean'."

Jackson came up with the groove on his drum machine at home. "I knew it was going to be big while I was writing it," Jackson wrote in his autobiography, Moonwalk. "I was really absorbed in that song." He was so consumed by the track while he was driving his Rolls Royce down the Ventura Freeway in Los Angeles that he didn't notice his car was on fire.

Jones says the song was about a stalker who climbed over Jackson's wall. "He woke up one morning and she was laying out by the pool, bathing suit on," said Jones. "And Michael says she had accused him of being the father of one of her twins."

Jackson unveiled "Billie Jean" – along with his moonwalk – to most of the world at a televised special celebrating the 25th anniversary of Motown Records. It was an instant sensation, and spent seven weeks at the #1 spot. For L.A. Reid and thousands of others, it's still the gold standard of dance pop. "Every day," Reid said, "I look for that kind of song."

BILLIE JEAN

Michael Jackson

She was More like beauty Queen
from a Movie scene I said Don't
mind but what do you mean I am the one
who will dance on the floor in the Round
she said I am the one who will dance
on the floor in the Round

she told Me her name was billie Jean
as he she caused a scene then every head
turned with eyes that dreamed of being the
one who will Dance on the floor in the Round
people always told Me be careful what you
Do don't go around breaking young girls
heart Mother always told Me
be careful who you love be careful what
you Do cause a lie becomes the truth.

chorus
Billie Jean is not My lover she is just a girl
who claims that I am the one. the kid is
not My Son, she says I am the one the kid is
Not My Son

STEVIE RAY VAUGHAN

"Pride and Joy"

"He was one of a kind," Dr. John said about Stevie Ray Vaughan. "You don't get many, and you better appreciate them while you still have them around." In his day, Stevie Ray Vaughan was saluted for his killer blues leads and highly rhythmic style – but he was also sometimes dismissed because he was too respectful of blues traditions and seemed not to break any new ground.

Now that he is gone (he died in a helicopter crash in 1990) his legacy is clear: he was a true heir to Jimi Hendrix's style of guitar, and a soulful performer who has inspired a generation of young players from Derek Trucks to John Mayer.

"Pride and Joy" was one of Vaughan's first truly spellbinding songs – an effortless display of his fluid style that could have been recorded any time in the last four decades. As the story goes, it was originally written for a girlfriend of Vaughan's; he later changed the words for his wife Lenora. She resented the fact that he hadn't originally written the song for her, so Vaughan reverted to the old lyrics. (Lenora got her own song, "Lenny.")

In 1994, Vaughan's hometown of Austin, Texas erected a statue of him on Lady Bird Lake, where he played a number of shows. It has become one of the city's most popular tourist attractions.

MADONNA
HOLIDAY

MADONNA "Holiday"

Madonna had a record deal when she recorded "Holiday," but she did not yet have a bank account. Within nine months, she was a household name. She was finishing her debut album Madonna in April 1983 and needed another song. Her boyfriend and co-conspirator, John "Jellybean" Benitez, found "Holiday," a track written by Curtis Hudson and Lisa Stevens of the group Pure Energy, which Mary Wilson of the Supremes had turned down.

Madonna and Benitez set to work on the track; she quickly recorded the vocals, and the duo spent days personalizing it, pulling in musician Fred Zarr to add a piano solo. "Holiday" came out in time for Thanksgiving 1983, getting a boost from the holiday season and taking off from there. "Holiday was as infectious as the plague," wrote Madonna biographer Rikky Rooksby. "For a few months in 1984 it seemed like you couldn't possibly escape this record. You could go hiking in Vancouver, chase kangaroos in the outback or mingle with the crowds in Bombay, and it seemed you'd still hear Madonna's shrill cry of 'it would

be so nice'!!"

Madonna has since called the songwriting on her first album "pretty weak," dismissing it as her "aerobics album," but "Holiday" can still get any room with dance party potential moving. Most important, it launched the biggest star of the last twenty-five years. In January 1984, Madonna went on the show American Bandstand to perform "Holiday" for her first nationwide TV appearance; when announcer Dick Clark asked her what she wanted to do when she grew up, she replied, "Rule the world."

Everybody spread the word
We're gonna have a celebration
All across the world
In every nation
It's time for the good times
Forget about the bad times, oh yeah
One day to come together
To release the pressure
We need a holiday

1984

"JUMP"

VAN HALEN

219 - David Lee Roth and Eddie Van Halen in 1984. The band was feuding over Eddie's use of a keyboard in "Jump."

"Jump" was where two great streams of Eighties pop – arena metal and synth rock – converged. It was also a turning point for Van Halen: their first #1 single, and the beginning of the end for singer David Lee Roth. There was tension in the band because guitar master Eddie Van Halen had built a studio in his home and was recording material there by himself, which brash singer Roth didn't like. One song Eddie came up with was the tune to "Jump" – the first Van Halen song ever to feature a synth lead.

Roth and producer Ted Templeman didn't like "Jump," according to Eddie: "I said, 'take it or leave it'. I was getting sick of their ideas of what was commercial." Templeman said, "'Jump' was recorded at Ed's studio ... in the middle of the night. Dave wrote the lyrics that afternoon in the backseat of his Mercury convertible. We finished all vocals that afternoon and mixed it that evening."

Roth has told a few different stories about his lyrics, but the most credible one is that he saw a TV news story about a man about to jump off a high ledge and kill himself – hence the line, "Might as well jump."

The band would enjoy enormous MTV play for "Jump," plus multiple other hits from 1984. But Roth was already halfway out the door, recording a solo EP, Crazy from the Heat. "At first Crazy from the Heat was great because Roth laid off me a bit," Van Halen said. "Little did I know he was testing the waters." After years apart, there was some sort of happy ending: Roth and Van Halen reunited for a tour in 2007.

I get up, and nothing gets me down./i like to jump. and then go round and round/And I know, just how it feels./You've got to roll with the

220 - Van Halen's "Jump" mixed 1970s hard rock and 1980's synth-pop.

221 - Van Halen in concert; shortly after the album "1984," David Lee Roth would leave the band.

punches to get to what's real/Oh can't you see me standing here, I'm getting ready for a soccer scene I ain't the worst that you've seen.

223 - Prince's "Purple Rain" album marked his commercial peak.

PRINCE
Nr.1 in USA

When doves cry

1984

PRINCE
"When Doves Cry"

"'When Doves Cry' is one of the most radical number one songs of the past twenty years," said Ahmir "Questlove" Thompson of the Roots. Deeply funky, a little odd and sexy as all hell, "Doves" didn't quite fit in with the rest of his landmark album, Purple Rain: Prince recorded most of Rain with his band the Revolution, but he recorded "When Doves Cry" by himself at Sunset Sound studios in Los Angeles. You can hear the difference: "Doves" sounds a little more closed in and doesn't have the earthy feel of tracks like "Let's Go Crazy" – it speaks to a different part of the listener's brain, the off-kilter psychological side.

"In the mix stage," his engineer, David Rivkin, told Rolling Stone, "Prince goes through another metamorphosis and says, 'We don't need this, we don't need that' and starts pulling off shit, that's how it works." In this case, he removed the song's bass line and a string section, giving it an otherworldly feel. Rivkin said his label, Warner Brothers, was nervous about "Doves": "They were a little afraid. They didn't know what to do with it because it was drastically different, but that's the way Prince always is. He does not copy himself."

"My goal is to excite and provoke on every level," said Prince. "I would rather give the people what they need rather than what they want." It turns out that the people both wanted and needed "When Doves Cry": it held the #1 spot for five weeks.

Dig if you will the picture/Of you and I engaged in a kiss/The sweat of your body covers me/Can you my darling/Can you picture this? Dream if you can a courtyard/An ocean of violets in bloom/Animals strike curious poses/They feel the heat

224 - Prince in concert at the Rosemont Horizon in Chicago, Illinois.

225 - Prince performs at the Nassau Coliseum in Long Island, New York.

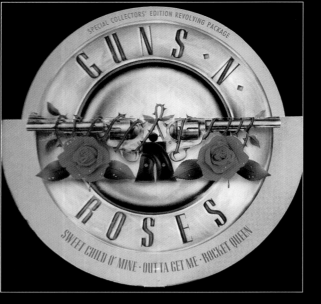

227 - The return of hard rock: Guns 'N Roses helped usher out hair metal with "Appetite for Destruction."

"Sweet Child O' Mine"

GUNS N'ROSES

"Sweet Child O' Mine" cut through the hair metal and synth pop that was dominating Eighties MTV and radio like a machete; within a year, it seemed like every hard rock band in the world was trying to be Guns N' Roses.

"The thing about 'Sweet Child O' Mine'," said bassist Duff McKagan, "is that it was written in five minutes." Slash says the famous high-pitched riff wasn't supposed to be serious – according to him it was just "fucking around with an intro riff, making a joke." He and drummer Stephen Adler were jamming, and Slash started playing what he called a 'circus' melody. Meanwhile, Axl Rose was upstairs and started writing lyrics about his girlfriend, Erin Everly.

The famous "Where do we go" section at the end of the song was an accident as well: Producer Mike Clink suggested that some sort of breakdown at the end would be effective, but the band didn't know what to do. Axl Rose started saying "Where do we go? Where do we go now?" to himself, and band took it from there, using those lyrics. "Sweet Child O' Mine" hit #1 on the U.S. Billboard singles charts and made it onto the top 40 around the globe.

She's got a smile that it seems to me
Reminds me of childhood memories
Where everything
Was as fresh as the bright blue sky
Now and then when I see her face
She takes me away to that special place
And if I'd stare too long
I'd probably break down and cry

228 - Slash in action: Guns 'N Roses live at the Rock in Rio concert.

229 - Guns 'N Roses would suffer from Axl Rose's erratic behavior in the years to come.

1989

MADONNA
"Like a Prayer"

Madonna was turning 30 and ending her three-and-a-half-year marriage to Sean Penn; the legal reason was "irreconcilable differences," but Madonna songs such as "Till Death Do Us Part" – also from the Like a Prayer album – hinted at violence and alcohol abuse ("He takes a drink / She goes inside / He starts to scream / The vases fly ... I wish that it would change / But it won't if you don't"). The song "Like a Prayer" was Madonna's big, redemptive statement after all this personal chaos. She pulled

out all the stops, trading on her success to deliver a nearly six-minute opus with a gospel choir ending and Prince delivering some heavy, uncredited guitar playing. "I didn't have the censors on me in terms of emotions or music," she said. "I did take a lot more chances with this one, but obviously success gives you the confidence to do those things."

Of course, because this was Madonna, her "big redemptive statement" included a metaphor about oral sex ("I'm down on my

knees / I want to take you there"). "Like a Prayer" was her greatest song yet, intimate yet irresistible and uplifting. Madonna gave some credit to her partnership with producer Pat Leonard: "He's melancholic, and he is a classically trained musician with an incredible sense of melody," she told Rolling Stone. "We always come up with something interesting. We usually don't write frivolous songs, although we've done that, too. There's something magical about our writing."

"Like a Prayer" was partially debuted in a two-minute Pepsi ad featuring Madonna – the first time a major artist had done that. Then she released the video, which featured her dancing in front of burning crosses. Religious groups complained, and Pepsi, spooked, pulled the commercial. (It ran only once.) "I like the challenge of mixing art and commerce," she said. Once again she had done it brilliantly; "Like a Prayer" shot to the top of the singles charts and would sell five million copies in short order.

1991

ENTER SANDMAN

METALLICA
"Enter Sandman"

Metallica were in a position to be bigger than ever as the 1990s arrived; they were coming off the thundering, multiplatinum And Justice for All – their fourth album and one of their most commercially successful yet. But they wanted to go even further. Talking about their underground status, drummer Lars Ulrich said, "It was cool, but it also limited us."

As the band readied their follow-up, guitarist Kirk Hammett came up with a dark, bruising riff. Singer James Hetfield suggested extending it from two bars to four; it would become the basis of "Enter Sandman." "We wrote it in an afternoon," says Ulrich. "The whole intro, the verse, the bridge, the chorus – it's the same riff." When they entered the studio, producer Bob Rock turned the riff into what Hetfield called a "wall of guitars," the rhythm line layered three times over.

Ulrich said that "Sandman" became the "foundation, the guide to the whole record." But Hetfield took a while to write the lyrics to the track. He thought the song sounded too commercial; to offset that, he wrote a dark song about a family with "a huge horrible secret." At Ulrich and Rock's urging, he redid the lyrics, making them about sleep and nightmares. Hammett paid special attention to the wailing solo: "I think the solo is amazing in its own right," he said later. "It fits in perfectly and adds a different dimension to the music." The song would become Metallica's most important single: a perfect mix of huge guitars, metal attitude and an accessible melody. It entered the Top 40 – a first for them – and took them to a new level of fame. Before, "they were a garage band who were supposed to tour for the rest of their life and that was it," said Lonn Friend, the editor of the metal magazine RIP. Now, they were one of the biggest rock bands of the 1990s.

Something's wrong, shut the light
Heavy thoughts tonight
And they aren't of Snow White
Dreams of war
Dreams of liars
Dreams of dragons fire
And of things that will bite, yeah

234 - James Hetfield, Jason Newsted, Kirk Hammett and Lars Ulrich (left to right) in Chicago, 1989.

235 - Metal's hardest band: Newsted, Hetfield, and Hammett in Minneapolis, 1988.

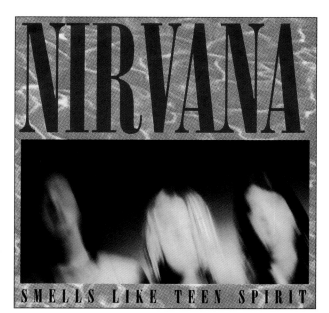

NIRVANA
"Smells Like Teen Spirit"

In the words of Rolling Stone's David Fricke, "Smells Like Teen Spirit" "wiped the lingering jive of the Eighties off the pop map." It's one of the few songs in rock that legitimately announced a new era: in this case, Nineties alternative rock.

Kurt Cobain allegedly got the title from his friend Kathleen Hanna of the band Bikini Kill, who wrote "Kurt Smells Like Teen Spirit" in spray paint on his wall. As the story goes, she was referring to a deodorant named Teen Spirit, but Cobain thought she was talking about rebellion and anarchy. "Nirvana really despised the mainstream," bassist Krist Novaselic said. "'Smells Like Teen Spirit' was all about the mass mentality of conformity."

Cobain came up with the song's central riff a few weeks before the band went into the studio to record their second album, Nevermind. Novaselic at first thought the riff was "ridiculous," and had the idea to slow it down during the verses. "I was trying to write the ultimate pop song," said Cobain, explaining, "I was basically trying to rip off the Pixies. I have to admit it. We used their sense of dynamics, being soft and quiet and then loud and hard."

When producer Butch Vig heard the band play "Teen Spirit" in rehearsals, it was "awesome sounding," he says. "I was pacing around the room, trying not to jump up and down in ecstasy." It became Nevermind's first single, although neither the record label nor the band thought it would be a big hit; the idea was that it would set the stage for "Come As You Are," the second single, to be a crossover. Instead, "Teen Spirit" muscled onto the charts, powered by a riveting MTV video featuring cheerleaders with anarchy symbols on their sweaters. Cobain claimed to have been befuddled, except for one thing: "I don't want to sound egotistical," he said, "but I know it's better than a majority of the commercial shit that's been crammed down people's throats for a long time."

With the lights out,
it's less dangerous
Here we are now,
entertain us
I feel stupid and
contagious
Here we are now,
entertain us

1992

RED HOT CHILI PEPPERS "Under the Bridge"

Red Hot Chili Peppers singer Anthony Kiedis had been a self-described "hardcore junkie" in the Eighties. His marriage to actress Ione Skye fell apart as a result, and, most devastatingly, his best friend and fellow heroin abuser, Chili Peppers guitarist Hillel Slovak, died of a drug overdose in 1988.

Kiedis had been clean for three years when the Chili Peppers prepared to record the album Blood Sugar Sex Magik with producer Rick Rubin. But the singer hadn't addressed any of his personal ordeals in a song. Then Rubin, visiting Kiedis to look at

his notebooks for song ideas, stumbled on the poem that would become "Under the Bridge." It contains lyrics like "Sometimes I feel like / I don't have a partner."

"What is this?" Rubin asked Kiedis. "Aw, that's not really a Chili Peppers song," Kiedis replied. "He never intended it for the band," Rubin said, adding, "I think that the Chili Peppers had put certain limitations mentally on what they thought they should be doing."

Rubin encouraged Kiedis to take the song to the rest of the band, who agreed that they should record it. It was the first true

ballad the band would record; still, they weren't sure about its commercial potential. "It doesn't really have a hook," said drummer Chad Smith, "and not to take away from Anthony, but he's not the greatest singer in the world. [His singing is] just cool and soulful. It's not the guy who wins all the awards, Michael Bolton."

But "Under the Bridge" was the most affecting song the Peppers had ever written; it surged up the U.S. charts and established them as one of the biggest bands of the decade. They were now more than just the punk-funk guys who took their shirts off.

I don't ever wanna feel like I did that day/Take me to the place I love, take me all the way/I don't ever wanna feel like /I did that day

242 - John Frusciante was the melodic force behind "Under the Bridge" and many more of the band's most successful songs.

243 - Singer Anthony Kiedis recounted his darkest days as a junkie in "Bridge."

Take me to the place I love, take me all the way/Under the bridge downtown/Is where I drew some blood/Under the bridge downtown. . .

"ONE"
1992
U2

245 - The members of U2 have said the band was on the brink of disintegration during the recording of "Achtung Baby."

It was looking like "this might be the end" of U2, according to drummer Larry Mullen Jr.: the band was in Berlin recording what would become the album Achtung Baby, and the sessions had stalled. The band was feuding over its creative direction and songs weren't coming together. Then the Edge played Bono two potential guitar parts for a section of the song "Mysterious Ways;" Bono liked one of them so much he wrote a new song around it. The lyrics "just fell out of the sky, a gift," Bono said, and "the melody, the structure – the whole thing was done in fifteen minutes."

The lyrics detail an uneasy relationship – "Did I disappoint you? / Leave a bad taste in your mouth?" – but end on a cautiously uplifting note ("We're one / But we're not the same / We get to carry each other.") "At the instant we were recording it, I got a very strong sense of its power," said the Edge. "We were all playing together in the big recording room, a huge, eerie ballroom full of ghosts of the war, and everything fell into place. It was a reassuring moment, when everyone finally went, 'Oh great, this album has started.'"

"One" became U2's greatest ballad; it also reassured the band that their songwriting process worked. People have interpreted the lyrics to be about everything from the band's feuding to German reunification. The Edge said "One" is a 'bitter, twisted, vitriolic conversation between two people who've been through some nasty, heavy stuff."

'It is a song about coming together, but it's not the old hippie idea of 'let's all live together'," said Bono. "It is, in fact, the opposite. It's not saying we even want to get along, but that we have to get along together in this world if it is to survive."

1995

OASIS
"Wonderwall"

It's Oasis' simplest ballad – nearly impossible to resist, even if many of the lyrics are close to impenetrable: "Today is gonna be the day / That they're gonna throw it back to you / By now you should've somehow / Realized what you gotta do." Noel, the band's guitarist and songwriter, has said he wrote "Wonderwall" about "an imaginary friend who's going to come and save you from yourself." ("Maybe / You're gonna be the one who saves me.") The title was taken from a 1968 soundtrack album by George Harrison.

"Wonderwall" was recorded in Wales, in less than eight hours. Producer Owen Morris says Noel came up with another arrangement of the song "which had some extra complicated bits that didn't have singing or melody but just had some chord changes – which seemed completely unnecessary," but was prevailed upon to keep the song simple.

"Wonderwall" became Oasis' biggest hit, reaching the #1 spot in the U.S. and Australia, among other countries, and #2 in the U.K. At some point, Noel said, the song was misinterpreted as being about his then-wife Meg Matthews. Gallagher said he had no choice but to play along: "The meaning of that song was taken away from me by the media who jumped on it. And how do you tell your Mrs. it's not about her once she's read it is?"

OK COMPUTER
RADIOHEAD

Lost Child

1997

RADIOHEAD
"Paranoid Android"

"Paranoid Android" started as an exercise: Radiohead wanted to write a song with three distinct, very different sections, like the Beatles' "Happiness is a Warm Gun." Different band members wrote the various parts, and the band started rehearsing. But they didn't have lyrics until Thom Yorke spent a long, unfortunate night at a Los Angeles club; he was surrounded by scenesters on cocaine, and a fight broke out. "The people I saw that night were just like demons from another planet," Yorke said. "Everyone was trying to get something out of me. I felt like my own self was collapsing in the presence of it,

but I also felt completely, utterly part of it, like it was all going to come crashing down any minute."

He wrote the lyrics when he got back to the hotel. "I was trying to sleep when I literally heard these voices that wouldn't leave me alone," he said. "They were the voices of the people I'd heard in the bar." The song takes its title from Marvin the Paranoid Android, a character in Douglas Adams' novel "The Hitchhiker's Guide to the Galaxy." The band began playing it live on tour while they were opening for Alanis Morrissette. At one point it ran more than ten minutes; Yorke would refer to it jokingly as their

"Pink Floyd cover." The version that ended up on their album OK Computer was six and a half minutes long, but still epic; despite its twists and turns, it ended up getting radio play, and charted in the U.K. It also signaled a new period for Radiohead – one less focused on the rock grandeur of The Bends, and more centered on wild experimentation. "It's the song that we played to our friends when they wanted to know what the new album was going to sound like," Colin Greenwood said. "You could see them thinking: 'If that's the new single, what will all the rest be like?'"

2003

YEAH, YEAH YEAHS
"Maps"

"Maps" could be the most wrenching love song of the last decade of rock: it's stark and moody, with a hauntingly repetitive refrain: "Maps / They don't love you like I love you." It was a mesmerizing change of pace for the Yeah Yeah Yeahs, who made their name in downtown New York with their explosive live shows and the onstage exploits of lead singer Karen O. As Nick Zinner delivered mighty, scratchy guitar riffs, Karen belted out songs in miniskirts, ripped T-shirts and fishnet stockings.

"Maps" is a song about Karen's ex-boyfriend, Angus Andrew of the New York band the Liars. (The title stands for 'My Angus please stay.') "There's a lot of love in that song," Karen O said. "But there's a lot of fear, too. I exposed myself so much with that song, I kind of shocked myself."

It took a while for "Maps" to find a place: the band's debut album, Fever to Tell, had sold only a little more than 100,000 copies when "Maps" was released as a single, and the band gained a dark horse nomination for a Grammy Award. With their label, Interscope Records, adding some marketing muscle – and the music video of Karen crying along spreading virally on the Internet – "Maps" eventually became a monster hit; since then, music publications such as Rolling Stone and NME have pronounced it one of the best songs of the 2000s.

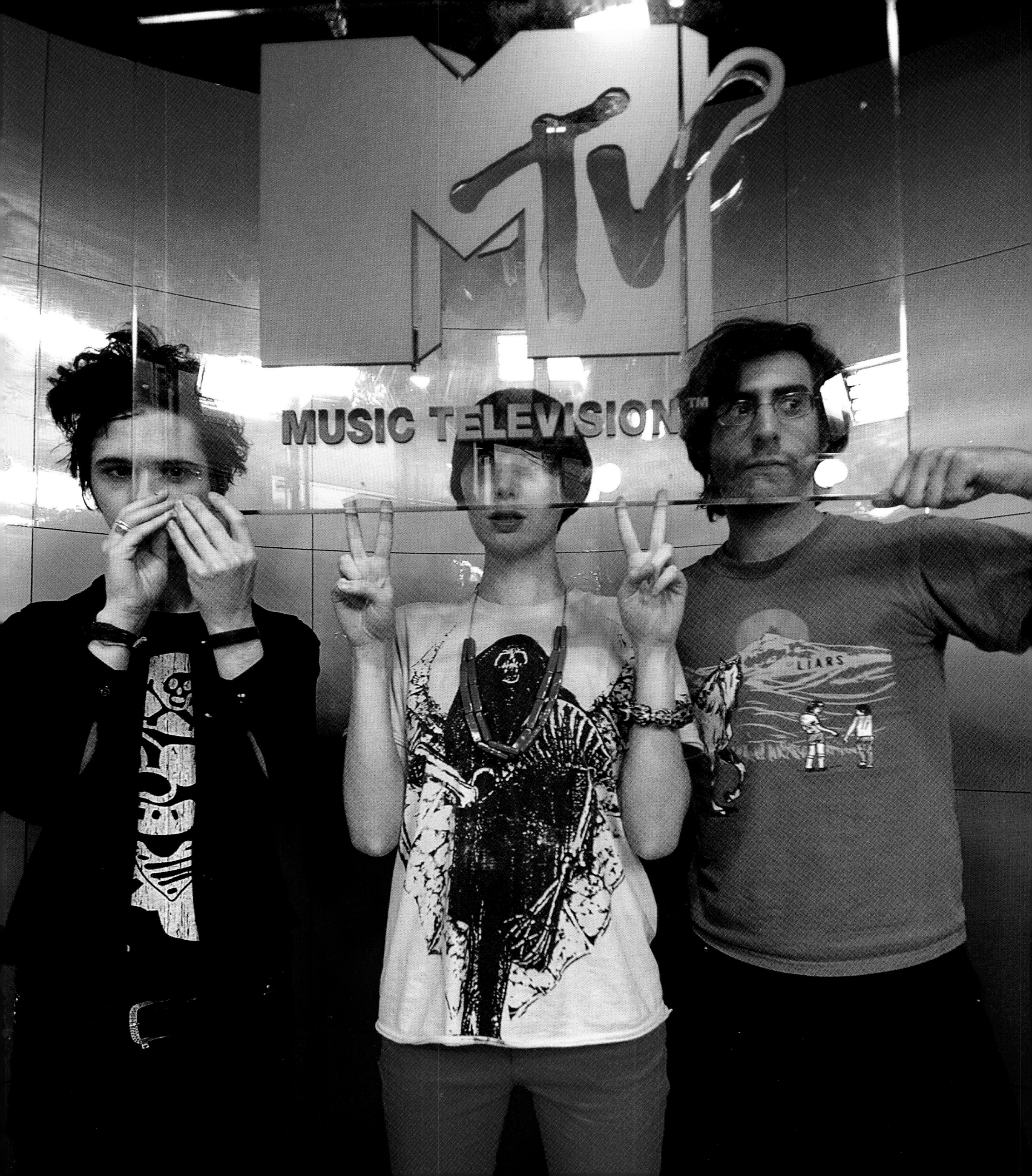
MUSIC TELEVISION
LIARS

Wait
They don't love you like I love you
Wait
They don't love you like I love you
Maps
Wait
They don't love you like I love you

254 - Along with the Strokes, the Yeah Yeah Yeahs put NewYork City back on the rock map in the early 2000s.

255 - One of rock's most riveting female performers: Karen O. at Lollapalooza in Chicago, Illinois.

2003

THE WHITE STRIPES
"7 Nation Army"

Many rock bands aim to be about freedom and possibilities; Jack White said the White Stripes are defined by their limitations — sticking to "vocals, guitars, drums; melody storytelling and rhythm; red, white and black."

"The whole idea of the band is that it was all about what not to do," White explained: "Why be repetitive? Why have two guitar players? Why have a bass player playing the same thing a guitar is playing? Let's break this down as much as possible and have it still be rock and roll and show what two people can do."

With "Seven Nation Army," Jack and his ex-wife Meg White took this limited format to its natural extreme: a pounding beat, a surging riff, over a bass guitar line simulated with a guitar. The title came from Jack's childhood name for the Salvation Army, but "that song's about gossip," he said. "Seven Nation Army is about this character who is involved in the realm of gossip with his friends and family and is so enraged by it

that he wants to leave town. It's about me, Meg and the people we're dating. The world constantly tries to dissect people, chew them up and spit them out. We get that all the time."

Elephant, the album with "Seven Nation Army," would go on to sell three million copies in less than a year. The song would also go on to become a football chant, especially among Italian soccer fans during Italy's 2006 World Cup run. Jack White was delighted.

I'm gonna fight 'em off
A seven nation army
couldn't hold me back
They're gonna rip it off
Taking there time right
behind my back

258 - According to the White Stripes, Jack and Meg White were brother and sister; in fact, they were once married, then separated.

259 - The White Stripes spurred a renewed interest in American blues and roots music.

2004

"American Idiot"

GREEN DAY

261 - Green Day in 2004: "American Idiot" was the most ambitious project they had ever embarked on.

It was every band's worst nightmare: Green Day had finished an entire album, to be titled Cigarettes and Valentines, which had gone missing. The master tracks were nowhere to be found. The band – leadman Billie Joe Armstrong, drummer Tre Cool and bassist Mike Dirnt – considered rerecording the songs, but producer Rob Cavallo asked them if they truly thought those songs represented their best work. The band "couldn't honestly look at ourselves and say, 'That was the best thing we've ever done'," said Armstrong, "So we decided to move on and do something completely new."

They spend three months writing new material; the first song they wrote was "American Idiot," one of their best ever. It was a scathing attack on the cowboy attitude of the Bush era, sporting some of the band's most brutal guitars. "We were like, 'Let's just go balls-out on the guitar sound – plug in the Les Pauls and Marshalls and let it rip'," Armstrong said. The idea for the lyrics came when Billie Joe heard the proudly redneck Lynyrd Skynyrd song "That's How I Like It" on the radio: "It was like, I'm proud to be a redneck," Armstrong said, "and I was like, oh my God, why would you be proud of something like that? This is exactly what I'm against." The band hit a chord: the album American Idiot would sell six million copies in the U.S. alone.

262/263 - Billie Joe Armstrong was reacting against the nationalism of George W. Bush's America with "Idiot."

Welcome to a new kind
of tension.
All across the alien nation.
Where everything isn't
meant to be okay.
Television dreams of tomorrow.
We're not the ones who're
meant to follow.
For that's enough to argue.

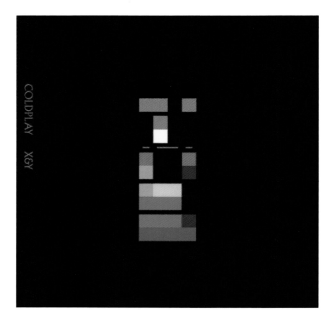

COLDPLAY XGY

2005

COLDPLAY "Fix You"

265 - Coldplay live at Madison Square Garden in New York City in 2006.

266/267 - Chris Martin in 2006: Coldplay spearheaded a return to smooth, uplifting melodies in rock radio.

It's one of Coldplay's most uplifting ballads, a message of hope and encouragement – "Lights will guide you home / And ignite your bones / And I will try to fix you" – over a swelling organ that builds to a rocking crescendo. According to Coldplay's singer Chris Martin, the song started with a sad event, the death of the father of Martin's wife, Gwyneth, and a discovery: "My father-in-law Bruce Paltrow bought this big keyboard just before he died," Martin said.

"No one had ever plugged it in. I plugged it in, and there was this incredible sound I'd never heard before. All these songs poured out from this one sound."

Bassist Guy Berryman said "Fix You" also takes some inspiration from Jimmy Cliff's classic "Many Rivers to Cross." It peaked at #59 on the Billboard charts; it was also the central part of a 2005 EP that went to benefit victims of Hurricane Katrina. Martin called it "probably the most important song we've ever written."

Index

Photo Credits

Page 13 David Redfern/Redferns/Getty Images
Page 15 CBS Photo Archive/Getty Images
Page 17 Michael Ochs Archives/Getty Images
Page 18 Michael Ochs Archives/Getty Images
Page 19 Bob Thomas/Pepperfoto/Getty Images
Page 21 Michael Ochs Archives/Getty Images
Page 23 Michael Ochs Archives/Corbis
Pages 24-25 Tony Frank/Sygma/Corbis
Page 27 Michael Ochs Archives/Getty Images
Page 29 David Redfern/Redferns/Getty Images
Pages 30-31 Express Newspapers/Getty Images
Page 33 Michael Ochs Archives/Getty Images
Page 35 David Redfern/Redferns/Getty Images
Page 37 Michael Ochs Archives/Corbis
Page 39 Michael Ochs Archives/Getty Images
Pages 40-41 Michael Ochs Archives/Getty Images
Page 43 Mirrorpix
Pages 44-45 Michael Ochs Archives/Getty Images
Page 46 Blank Archives/Hulton Archive/Getty Images
Page 47 Van Wilmer/Redferns/Getty Images
Pages 48-49 Michael Ochs Archives/Getty Images
Page 51 Michael Ochs Archives/Getty Images
Page 52 Michael Ochs Archives/Getty Images
Page 53 David Redfern/Redferns/Getty Images
Page 54 Jan Persson/Redferns/Getty Images
Page 55 Jan Persson/Redferns/Getty Images
Page 57 David Redfern/Redferns/Getty Images
Page 59 Michael Ochs Archives/Getty Images
Page 61 Victor Blackman/Express/Getty Images
Page 63 Michael Ochs Archives/Getty Images
Page 65 Petra Niemeier - K&K/Redferns/Getty Images
Page 67 William James Warren/Science Faction/Corbis
Page 69 Joel Brodsky/Corbis
Page 70 Michael Ochs Archives/Getty Images
Page 71 Joel Brodsky/Corbis
Page 73 Michael Ochs Archives/Getty Images
Page 75 Mick Gold/Redferns/Getty Images
Pages 76-77 Steve Schapiro/Corbis
Page 79 Petra Niemeier - K&K/Redferns/Getty Images
Pages 80-81 Michael Ochs Archives/Getty Images
Page 83 Odd Andersen/AFP/Getty Images
Page 85 Michael Ochs Archives/Getty Images
Page 87 Henry Diltz/Corbis
Page 89 Michael Ochs Archives/Getty Images
Page 90 Keystone Features/Getty Images
Page 91 Michael Ochs Archives/Getty Images
Page 93 Michael Ochs Archives/Getty Images
Page 95 David Redfern/Redferns/Getty Images
Page 97 Chris Walter/WireImage/Getty Images
Page 98 Henry Diltz/Corbis
Page 99 Chris Walter/WireImage/Getty Images
Page 100 Chris Walter/WireImage/Getty Images
Page 101 Chris Walter/WireImage/Getty Images
Page 103 David Redfern/Redferms/Getty Images
Page 105 Michael Ochs Archives/Getty Images
Page 106 Chris Walter/WireImage/Getty Images
Page 107 Neal Preston/Corbis

Page 109 Elliott Landy/Redferns/Getty Images
Page 110 Jan Persson/Redferns/Getty Images
Page 111 Tom Copi/ Michael Ochs Archives/Getty Images
Page 112 Michael Ochs Archives/Stringer/Getty Images
Page 113 Neal Preston/Corbis
Pages 114-115 Neal Preston/Corbis
Page 117 Tom Copi/ Michael Ochs Archives/Getty Images
Page 119 Neal Preston/Corbis
Pages 120-121 Bettmann/Corbis
Page 123 Gijsbert Hanekroot/Redferns/Getty Images
Page 125 Debi Doss/Hulton Archive/Getty Images
Pages 126-127 Neal Preston/Corbis
Page 129 Gijsbert Hanekroot/Redferns/Getty Images
Page 131 Michael Ochs Archives/Getty Images
Pages 132-133 Michael Artault/Apis/Sygma/Corbis
Page 133 Jeff Albertson/Corbis
Page 135 Michael Ochs Archives/Getty Images
Page 136 Jorgen Angel/ Redferns/Getty Images
Page 137 Chris Walter/WireImage/Getty Images
Page 139 Michael Ochs Archives/Getty Images
Page 141 Graham Wood/Evening Standard/Getty Images
Page 143 Neal Preston/Corbis
Page 145 Anwar Hussein/Hulton Archive/Getty Images
Page 147 Neal Preston/Corbis
Page 148 Richard McCaffrey/Michael Ochs Archive/ Getty Images
Pages 148-149 Richard McCaffrey/Michael Ochs Archive/Getty Images
Page 151 Jeff Albertson/Corbis
Page 152 Tom Hill/WireImage/Getty Images
Page 153 SGranitz/WireImage/Getty Images
Page 155 George Tiedemann/Corbis
Page 157 Richard E. Aaron/Redferns/Getty Images
Page 158 Andrew Putler/Redferns/Getty Images
Page 159 Andrew Putler/Redferns/Getty Images
Page 161 Ian Dickson/Redferns/Getty Images
Pages 162-163 Andrew Putler/ Redferns/Getty Images
Page 165 Michael Ochs Archives/Getty Images
Page 167 Janette Beckman/Getty Images
Pages 168-169 Kevin Cummins/Getty Images
Page 171 Neal Preston/Corbis
Page 172 Richard McCaffrey/ Michael Ochs Archives /Getty Images
Page 173 Andrew Putler/Redferns/Getty Images
Pages 174-175 David Redfern/Redferns/Getty Images
Page 177 Mark Sullivan/Getty Images
Page 178 Howard Barlow/Redferns/Getty Images
Page 179 Steve Emberton/Getty Images
Page 181 Gerard Rancinan/Sygma/Corbis
Pages 182-183 Lynn Goldsmith/Corbis
Page 185 Michael Ochs Archives/Getty Images
Page 186 Larry Hulst/Michael Ochs Archive/Getty Images

Page 187 Michael Ochs Archives/Getty Images
Page 189 Phil Dent/Redferns/Getty Images
Page 191 Roger Ressmeyer/Corbis
Pages 192-193 Roger Ressmeyer/Corbis
Page 195 Roberta Bayley/Redferns/Getty Images
Page 197 Lorne Resnick/Redferns/Getty Images
Pages 198-199 Lorne Resnick/Redferns/Getty Images
Page 201 Michael Ochs Archive/Getty Images
Page 203 Express Newspapers/Getty Images
Page 204 Terry O'Neill/Getty Images
Page 205 A&M Records/Getty Images
Page 207 Ebet Roberts/Redferns/Getty Images
Pages 208-209 Lynn Goldsmith/Corbis
Page 210 Richard Corkery/New York Daily News Archive/Getty Images
Page 211 Astrid Stawiarz/Getty Images
Page 213 Clayton Call/Redferns/Getty Images
Page 215 Deborah Feingold/Corbis
Page 217 Deborah Feingold/Corbis
Page 219 Andy Freeberg/Getty Images
Page 220 Michael Ochs Archives/Getty Images
Page 221 Neal Preston/Corbis
Page 223 Ebet Roberts/Redferns/Getty Images
Page 224 Richard E. Aron/Redferns/Getty Images
Page 225 Ebet Roberts/Redferns/Getty Images
Page 227 Kevin Mazur/WireImage/Getty Images
Page 228 Neal Preston/Corbis
Page 229 Kevin Mazur/WireImage/Getty Images
Page 231 Frank Micelotta/ImageDirect/Getty Images
Page 233 Tim Mosenfelder/ImageDirect/Getty Images
Page 234 Paul Natkin/WireImage/Getty Images
Page 235 Jim Steinfeldt/Michael Ochs Archives/Getty Images
Page 237 Joe Giron/Corbis
Pages 238-239 Michel Linssen/Redferns/Getty Images
Page 241 Paul Natkin/WireImage/Getty Images
Page 242 Ian Dickson/Redferns/Getty Images
Page 243 Stuart Mostyn/Redferns/Getty Images
Page 245 Neal Preston/Corbis
Page 246 Andrew Fox/Corbis
Page 247 Mick Hutson/Redferns/Getty Images
Page 249 Kevin Cummins/Getty Images
Page 251 Bob Berg/Getty Images
Page 253 Nayan Sthakiya/Corbis
Page 254 Brian Hineline/Retna Ltd./Corbis
Page 255 Rob Grabowski/Retna Ltd./Corbis
Page 257 Tim Mosenfelder/Corbis
Page 258 Jean Baptiste Lacroix/WireImage/Getty Images
Page 259 R. Diamond/WireImage/Getty Images
Page 261 Denise Truscello/WireImage/Getty Images
Pages 262-263 Kevin Mazur/WireImages/Getty Images
Page 265 Mick Hutson/Redferns/Getty Images
Pages 266-267 Mick Hutson/Redferns/Getty Images

NATHAN BRACKETT is a deputy managing editor at Rolling
Stone. He served as the editor of RollingStone.com from 2007-
2009, and is the editor of Rolling Stone's "500 Greatest Songs of
All Time" (2010). He has commented on music for ABC's Good
Morning America, CNN, MSNBC, Inside Edition, VH1, MTV and
many other networks. He lives in Brooklyn, NY with his wife and
two children.

The publisher wish to tank:
RED MOON of Walter Pettorosso

WHITE STAR PUBLISHERS

WS White Star Publishers® is a registered trademark
property of Edizioni White Star s.r.l.

© 2011 Edizioni White Star s.r.l.
Via Candido Sassone, 24
13100 Vercelli, Italia
www.whitestar.it

ISBN 978-88-544-0582-0

1 2 3 4 5 6   15 14 13 12 11

Printed in China